A Revolutionary Princess
Christina Belgiojoso-Trivulzio

THE PRINCESS BELGIOJOSO

A Revolutionary Princess
Christina Belgiojoso-Trivulzio

An Italian Noble Woman's Struggle for Italian Independence in the 19th Century

H. Remsen Whitehouse

LEONAUR

A Revolutionary Princess Christina Belgiojoso-Trivulzio
An Italian Noble Woman's Struggle for Italian Independence in the 19th Century
by H. Remsen Whitehouse

First published under the title:
A Revolutionary Princess Christina Belgiojoso-Trivulzio

Leonaur is an imprint of Oakpast Ltd

Copyright in this form © 2017 Oakpast Ltd

ISBN: 978-1-78282-666-8 (hardcover)
ISBN: 978-1-78282-667-5 (softcover)

http://www.leonaur.com

Publisher's Notes

Contents

To
My Brother
J. Norman Whitehouse

Preface

The materials for this study have been gleaned from many sources. Official documents and private correspondence in the libraries of Milan, Florence, and Paris have been carefully examined, and contemporary memoirs in Italian, French, and English freely utilised.

To acknowledge individually my many obligations to friends in Italy and France would tax the patience of my readers. I wish, however, to make known my special indebtedness to the Commendatore Raffaello Barbiera, an Italian biographer of the Princess Belgiojoso, whose patient investigations and minute studies of the social and political undercurrents of Milanese local history have been of inestimable value, not only as indications of the route to be followed, but in facilitating the laborious task of winnowing the chaff from the grain amidst discouraging piles of official records.

To His Excellency the Commendatore Senator Malvano, General Secretary of the Ministry of Foreign Affairs in Rome, whose influence procured me unrestricted access to the Lombard Secret Archives preserved in Milan, I tender most cordial thanks.

My debt to Mr. William Roscoe Thayer, of Cambridge, Mass., for valuable criticism and advice, is a heavy one.

Nor can I refrain from expressing my gratitude, for assistance rendered in procuring illustrations for the book, to the Marchesa Peruzzi de Medici, to Count Max Michiel, to Miss Florence Forbes, and to Mr. Sydney Schiff.

H. Remsen Whitehouse.

Villa Denantou, Ouchy.
July, 1906.

Introductory

Princess Belgiojoso left no private or personal record of her eventful life. Her very considerable literary baggage, dealing almost exclusively with political and sociological problems, affords but rare and fleeting glimpses of the author's inner self; while of her private correspondence very little is accessible. Her biographer consequently finds himself constrained to draw upon the (fortunately) numerous memoirs of French and Italian contemporaries, most of whom, however, confine themselves to casual mention of her eccentricities or expressions of unbounded admiration of her ardent patriotism.

The voluminous correspondence of the secret agents of the Austrian Government, who for many years minutely chronicled her words and actions, are of course not without their value; but it should be borne in mind that these reports were the work of spies whose means of livelihood depended on their skill in fostering and stimulating the suspicions of their employers.

Few of the actors who flit across the stage of Italy's great drama of National Independence equal the Princess Belgiojoso in romantic interest—none surpass her. Although her role was a minor one, yet, ever and *anon*, she advanced to the footlights, mingling with the "stars," and forcibly arrested the attention of the audience, exciting not only curiosity, but creating the impression that hers was a figure of no mean significance in the development of plot and action.

Furthermore, for well-nigh half a century her name was a familiar one not alone in Italian political and patriotic circles, but to the ears of intellectual Europe.

"*Femina sexu, ingenio vir*," quotes Monselet in a contemporary sketch. (*Statues et Statuettes contemporaines*, Paris, 1851.) Within certain limits the aphorism is an acceptable definition of a temperament at once peculiarly feminine yet on which are grafted attributes supposedly distinctive of masculine genius alone. Womanlike, her reason was almost invariably subjective to sentiment and to transient emotion: she never stopped to determine of what stuff her dreams were made, and when disillusion outran optimism she readily reverted to the prerogatives of her sex.

Full of contradictory elements; lacking equilibrium, yet keenly sensitive to logical appreciations; above and beyond all, stubbornly tenacious of an abstract ideal, the mental processes of this essentially paradoxical nature baffle deductive analysis. Veiled in a haze of mystery, the halo of martyrdom poised over her lovely head, the personality of this strange woman—remarkable both despite and on account of her vagaries and extravagances—is of yet further interest as, in a sense, typical of the singular admixture of practical and visionary ideals prevailing during the evolutionary period of Italy's national regeneration.

Notwithstanding her eccentricities and exaggerations, this frail epileptic Milanese patrician, the daughter of one of the proudest aristocracies of Europe, undoubtedly wielded in her time an intellectual fascination as effective as it was far-reaching. At once a social heroine and a political martyr, her hold over a popular imagination gradually unfolding to the realisation of the patriotic ideals of which she was readily accepted as the incarnation, was, for a space at least, considerable. Her influence with the sterner minds which guided and shaped the revolutionary movements in Italy was by the very reason of her impetuosity more restricted, but all, at one time or another, experienced the magnetism of her enthusiasm.

Liberally endowed with the histrionic temperament, an audience was as essential to Christina Belgiojoso as the air she breathed. Yet when this has been confessed the worst stands revealed. The purity of her patriotism is but little affected by the egotism of her personal vanity, oftenest discernible under the guise of that harmless dramatic posturing which some of her detractors pretend is never dissociated from even the most signal of her achievements as a propagandist of political liberties.

Continually shocking the susceptibilities and outraging the conventionalities of an epoch not particularly conspicuous for good taste, this erratic social and political free-lance never forfeited the consideration due to her birth. Sincerely democratic in the best Italian interpretation of the term, all through her many metamorphoses, whether as a Mazzinian conspirator and Republican, an Albertist Liberal, or an independent Revolutionist, she jealously retained her title to the inherent privileges of a great lady. Even the "citizen" Belgiojoso scorned to forswear the aristocrat, and never omitted from her signature the prefix which was hers by "right divine."

Nor would this lapse from the tenets of the creed she embraced appear to have been in any way resented by her political co-religionaries. With the rank and file of revolutionary patriots, dazzled by the sublime audacity of her anti-Austrian intrigues and her open defiance of the mandates from Vienna, the sincerity of her democracy was unquestioned. But the princess was not content to cast her spell over any one element of the great national movement she sought to inspire. The charm and brilliancy of her conversation, the attraction of an intelligence ever on the alert, together with the originality and piquancy of her wit, caused her to be surrounded at home and abroad by all that was foremost in the world of fashion, politics, literature, and art.

Among the wives and daughters of the Lombard patriots who risked life, liberty, and fortune to free their country from the yoke of the foreigner, her exalted social position, her exceptional beauty, her wealth, hardly less than, the compelling magnetism of her fierce enthusiasm and singular independence of character, combined to assign to the Princess Belgiojoso conspicuous prominence. Feminine participation in the conspiracies and political intrigues of the early and middle years of the last century was by no means uncommon in Italy, especially in Lombardy, where the heel of the Austrian usurper ground hardest. But few rivalled this strenuous champion in the intensity of the hatred vouchsafed the foreign despotism which sought to enslave the intellectual and moral life of northern Italians, as it had bounded their political liberties.

Chapter 1

Foreign Domination in Italy

For generations Spaniard and Austrian disputed the domination of Italy. Each in turn left traces of political ascendency, but neither was ever successful in obliterating the feudal individualism which survived the Middle Ages; as effectively isolating Italians in various petty States as a barrier of Alps or sea. At the close of the eighteenth century, with but three exceptions, despots of foreign extraction sat upon the thrones of the Peninsula. The States of the Church were ruled by a theocratic Sovereign, an Italian by birth, but a cosmopolitan by virtue of the universality of the office he filled, and in frequent instances owing the exercise of his sovereignty to foreign intervention. In Piedmont, it is true, the dynasty was national; but the despotism and feudalism varied in degree only from those prevailing elsewhere.

Venice alone boasted a popular form of government—democratic in theory, but oligarchical in form and practice. The Napoleonic invasions of 1796 and 1801, and the republics and kingdoms arbitrarily founded by the Conqueror, not only effaced the old landmarks of political geography throughout Italy, but infused a spirit of national cohesion hitherto unknown. Moreover, under the French administration, based on the revolutionary and humanitarian principles of 1789, Italians for the first time enjoyed a semblance of political liberties. Napoleon has been called the founder of modern Italy. Certain it is that his creation, the Kingdom of Italy, organically incomplete and destined to destruction on his fall, arose Phoenix-like from the ashes under which smouldered the Genius of Nationality his administration had awakened.

Of this short-lived kingdom, Milan had been the brilliant capital. Hither the Emperor came (1805) in gorgeous state to circle his brow with the Iron Crown, which legend claims as fashioned from a nail of the Cross. Hither the Vice-Regal Court of Eugène de Beauharnais attracted ambitious politicians from all parts of Italy.

The destinies of the Lombard city had for a century past been chequered. Ceded to Austria by the terms of the Treaty of Utrecht (1713) on the termination of the War of the Spanish Succession, occupied by the Spanish and French (1745), recovered by the Austrians (1746), the Duchy remained an appanage of the Hapsburgs after the Peace of Aix-la-Chapelle until Napoleon's victorious descent into Italy (1796). For nearly a generation French influences moulded the thought of Northern Italy, awakening the first glimmering instincts of political and national ambitions. On the fall of Napoleon, the Congress of Vienna (1815) restored the domination of Austria, and the darkness of foreign despotism closed in once more, snuffing out the flickering spark of Nationalism it had been the policy of the great Emperor to fan.

Among the Milanese patricians attached to the Court of Eugène de Beauharnais the family of Trivulzio stood conspicuous. The aristocracy of Europe boasts no bluer blood than that which runs in the veins of this distinguished race, tracing descent from the twelfth century and numbering among its scions a marshal of France. As a chamberlain of the Vice-Regal Court the Marquis Jerome Trivulzio was in close touch with the stepson of the Emperor Napoleon, and being in sympathy with the French *régime* he readily consented to the appointment of his wife as a lady of honour to the Bavarian Princess selected as Eugène's consort.

To Jerome and Victoria Trivulzio was born, on June 28, 1808, a girl, who, among a long string of baptismal appellations (twelve in all) received that of Christina. This child, our heroine, first saw the light of day in Milan, and in the palace which for generations had sheltered her ancestors.

Jerome Trivulzio died in 1812, when his only child was barely four years old. The young mother, left a widow in her twenty-first year, soon after accepted the hand of the Marquis Alexander Visconti d'Aragona. This nobleman, belonging to an historical and illustrious house, also officially connected with the representatives of the Napoleonic *régime*, achieved for himself a lasting reputation for pure and unselfish patriotism by his unswerving devotion to the cause he later espoused.

Before Christina Trivulzio had attained her sixth year the abdication of Napoleon (April, 1814) completely transformed the political situation in Italy. The Vice-Regal Court was dispersed, Prince Eugène taking refuge within the dominions of his father-in-law, the King of Bavaria.

Sullenly the sympathisers with the French *régime* sought the seclusion of private life. Not, however, before a final attempt had been made to convince the Allied Sovereigns assembled in Paris of the anachronism a return to the political conditions prevailing prior to the French administration must involve. But all was in vain. The heavy hand of Austria immediately set about strangling the new-born Nationalism: the censorship was merciless towards any whose temerity led them to criticise unfavourably the conduct of public affairs; even literature, always provided it possessed no political significance, was tolerated rather than encouraged.

Yet, in spite of this frankly hostile atmosphere and the general intellectual stagnation it engendered, a few choice spirits survived, and braving the certain displeasure of their Imperial master, essayed the publication of the *Conciliatore* journal, which, notwithstanding its pacific name, was soon recognised as a war-cry in disguise. Count Federico Confalonieri, whom Madame de Stael claimed as representing with three of his contemporaries *l'Italie spirituelle toute entière,* was a guiding spirit of this hazardous venture.

Ostensibly a literary publication founded for purposes of popular education and the spread of philanthropic principles, it was in reality intended gradually to familiarise public sentiment with the ideals cherished by its editors. Speedily unmasked, it was ruthlessly suppressed towards the close of 1819; not, however, before the subtle poison of its cleverly edited essays had permeated deeply the *strata* of political apathy which overlay the embers of patriotism in the breast of many a Lombard dreamer. A few of the more prominent contributors, among others Silvio Pellico, the immortal author of *Le Mie Prigioni,* were arrested and thrown into jail; thus, inaugurating the long series of political persecutions which converted the boasted paternal rule of Austria into a veritable Reign of Terror.

The young stepfather of Christina Trivulzio had been connected with the *Conciliatore.* Although deeply compromised, for the time being he escaped arrest or molestation. His house continued to be the rendezvous of the artistic and literary celebrities of the day; but beneath the cloak of the Muses there peeped the shrinking figure of Conspiracy. Soon the social atmosphere of clubs and salons began to undergo a subtle change. Hitherto tainted with no heavier ingredients than scandal or the idle gossip emanating from the *foyer* of the opera, it was now not infrequently charged with sullen discontent. The new wine of Liberalism so heedlessly forced into the old bottles of Absolutism was beginning to ferment. As yet the explosions were isolated, amounting to little more than an evidence of the pent-up forces within; but as they increased in frequency they perceptibly jarred their neighbours, thus jeopardising the stability of the whole.

Before she was twelve years old Christina Trivulzio was conscious of the vague social unrest which surrounded her. Imperfectly formed patriotic aspirations already haunted her childish brain. Her education was entrusted to men conspicuous not only for their learning but for the broadness of their views, and, from an Austrian standpoint, the unorthodoxy of their political creeds. In her case the cramping prejudices of an aristocracy half Spanish in its traditions and its contempt for the mental development of women were cast aside. The young girl received an education which for variety of subject and thoroughness in detail would not compare unfavourably with the curriculum of the most noted women's colleges of our own day.

Inevitably she was saturated with the Classicism and Romanticism of the period, both finding in her temperamental peculiarities a fertile soil. But her strong leaning towards the practical and utilitarian application of politics in a measure counterbalanced her romantic conception of the purely ethical side of public affairs, although powerless to guarantee her from periodical attacks of the vapid sentimentalism so prevalent among intellectual women of her time. In after-life her knowledge of the science of government, although never profound, was comprehensive; while she possessed the gift, rare in a woman, of a just perspective when estimating a political situation.

Evidence of this is apparent in the remarkable articles published by her in the *Revue des Deux Mondes* (September 15 and October 1, 1848), barely five months after the memorable insurrection which afforded Milan temporary relief from Austrian oppression, but which also, owing to the jealousies and fierce rivalries it excited, went far towards arresting the development of Nationalism for a decade. Although she did not escape the pretentiousness invariably attaching to the *femme politique*, hers was never of a type common to the mistresses of *salons* where the humanism of politics is made subservient to rhetorical brilliancy. The guilelessness of her Latin democracy often prompted her to rush in where an Anglo-Saxon aristocrat would fear to tread. But, although the catholicity of her acquaintance was

PRINCE METTERINCH.

equalled only by the eclecticism of her enthusiasms, her motives were rarely misunderstood, except by her peers.

As has been intimated, Christina Trivulzio's childhood and early youth were passed in an atmosphere of active if suppressed political discontent. Not only her stepfather, but several blood relations, belonged to the little band of determined patriots who, without yet daring to advocate open rebellion, sought to inculcate among the masses that spirit of Nationalism which could alone prevail against the widespread Austrian supremacy in Italy.

It was at that time, as indeed it continued to be, the Machiavellian policy of Prince Metternich to lull the restiveness of enforced inaction and blunt the inconvenient political aspirations of the Emperor's Milanese subjects, by the encouragement of facile, enervating pleasures. The great Chancellor readily perceived that the danger to a successful denationalisation of the annexed Italian provinces lay not with the ignorant masses, whose plodding routine and daily struggle for bare material existence left them apathetic towards the ethical aspect of their political status, but with the educated classes.

To these latter the Liberal principles of the French *régime* had opened careers and legitimised political ambitions hitherto unknown, opportunities of which the more progressive and intelligent members of the aristocracy hardly less than of the professional classes had hastened to avail themselves. In spite of the shifting and transitory character of the Napoleonic era, its homogeneity, contrasted with the warring dynastic interests to which Italians were accustomed, prepared the ground for the seed of a slow-growing national spirit. It was the fostering and development of this tender plant which the *Conciliatore*, with its able staff, had undertaken, and which, despite persecution, a devoted band of patriotic intellectualists proposed to carry on. Notwithstanding the temptations besetting a man of his social and financial position in a gay and pleasure-loving city such as Milan, and the indulgence with which dissipation of all kinds was viewed, the Marquis d'Aragona, while leading the life of a member of the fashionable world, never lost sight of the patriotic obligations he had assumed.

Under existing conditions these could only be furthered by resort to conspiracy, that doubtfully efficient but universal weapon of the weak in dealing with forces numerically or organically superior. With the suppression of the *Conciliatore* a stunning blow had been aimed at the pioneers of a popular intellectual movement. Now, even those who directed their efforts towards the development of the material welfare of their fellow-citizens were to come under the ban. As in Russia today, (1906), philanthropy was frowned upon as constituting a danger to the State. Likewise, the introduction of gas for lighting the streets, and the experimental navigation by steam on the River Pô, met with stern disapproval. Machinery of any kind excited deep suspicion, being speedily recognised as a revolutionary force transforming not merely economic, but social conditions, and that to the detriment of the established order.

In every innovation Austria detected a foe. As the years went by every innovator, whether working on spiritual, intellectual, political, or purely material lines, was treated as an enemy, hounded by spies and the ubiquitous police, driven into exile, or rendered innocuous behind prison bars. As a consequence, few of the youthful aristocrats ventured to raise themselves above the mediocrity of their caste, while professional men, with rare exceptions, contented themselves with following the beaten track of custom. Not so, however, the young and enterprising d'Aragona, whose participation in several of the above-mentioned schemes had caused his name to be writ large in the black books of the civic authorities, and who was shrewdly suspected of disaffection of an even more serious character.

Baulked in their role of pacific educators of the popular mind, conspiracy constituted the only safety-valve for the explosive passions of the political malcontents. To conspire against his enemy is as instinctive with the Italian as is the impulsive resort to his fists to an Anglo-Saxon. Through all the centuries of Italian social history it has been the consecrated weapon of the oppressed in their revolt against the oppressor. Secret societies, such as the Carbonaria and Adelphia, both with more or less acknowledged Republican tendencies, extended their ramifications not only throughout the Peninsula, but in France and Germany as well. Lombardy sheltered many adherents to these sects, and had, moreover, given birth to local societies professing similar creeds. The most important, founded and directed by Count Confalonieri, a moving spirit of chronic and uncompromising hostility towards the Austrian *régime*, was called the *Federazione*. To this association the Marquis d'Aragona had sought initiation.

The ideals professed by the *Federati* would appear to have been as nebulous as those of other societies of like sort until the grant of a constitution to the Neapolitans, followed by the military revolt in Piedmont and the abdication of King Victor Emmanuel I. (March, 1821) inspired more concrete aims.

It is beside our purpose to enter into the details of this plot, although its far-reaching influences deeply tinged the political situation in Lombardy. The heir to the throne of Piedmont, Prince Charles Albert, was supposed to be in sympathy, if not active collusion, with the leaders of the *Federati*, and when he was entrusted with a temporary Regency in Piedmont it was believed that the moment for action had arrived. But although Charles Albert promptly granted a constitution, he wavered when an invasion of Lombardy was urged, and ultimately, he submitted tamely to the decree of exile pronounced against him by the new king, Charles Felix.

The Marquis Pallavicino, a cousin of our young heroine, who had taken an active part in the seditious intrigue, soon fell into the trap laid for him by the Austrian police. Other arrests followed, among those cast into prison being Confalonieri and the Marquis d'Aragona.

To Christina Trivulzio were now first brought home the horrors of that political tyranny towards the destruction of which all the powers of her exceptional intelligence were to be lavished during her long and eventful career. Although but thirteen years of age, the sensational arrest and dramatic trial of her beloved stepfather, the Marquis d'Aragona, made an indelible impression on the mind and character of the sensitive child.

The Marchesa d'Aragona had but just set out on her afternoon drive when an acquaintance whispered in her ear that the houses of her husband's political friends were being searched. Retaining her presence of mind, she ordered her coachman to change his route and drive to a neighbouring country house where she knew d'Aragona kept compromising papers. Once beyond the precincts of the fashionable promenade, the horses were lashed to a gallop, for she realised that not a moment was to be lost if she would place her husband in a position of comparative safety. To tear open drawers and closets and to burn every scrap of paper she could lay hands on, was the work of but a few moments.

When the police arrived, the smoke was still curling up the chimney, but every atom of incriminating evidence was destroyed. In spite of his wife's precautionary action, however, the Marquis d'Aragona was immediately arrested and held on the charge of high treason, conviction of which meant death. The capture of Confalonieri was particularly dramatic. His political heresies being an open secret, for years he had been closely watched by Austrian agents at home and abroad. Seven months before his arrest the count, writing to Gino Capponi concerning the many arrests made throughout Lombardy and Venetia on suspicion of connivance with the Piedmontese rising, exclaims:

Among all these (who would have believed it!) the only one remaining if not unsuspected at least unmolested is myself.

But he knew that the calm was only apparent, and that he would soon find himself in troubled waters.

I know it: I am prepared for it: I fear nothing, and I will not move to avoid it. It is not unknown to you with what persistence the starveling police buzz round me; but I laugh at the vile tribunal: as long as opinions and abstract theories are not accounted crimes their manoeuvres cannot avail against me.

Was it all bombast? Did the arrogant aristocrat really believe himself invulnerable, and that, failing tangible proof of his personal participation in the plot to oust Austria, the emperor himself would hesitate to molest one of his exalted social standing? No documents of an incriminating character were ever discovered; the evidence on which he was held was purely circumstantial. Yet, such as it was, it sufficed to convince the judges that he deserved the death penalty: a sentence which the clemency of the emperor commuted to life imprisonment in the dread Spielberg.

Nor, in spite of his vaunted assurance, had Confalonieri neglected means whereby to make good his escape in case of threatened arrest. Calm and confident when eventually face to face with his captors, the count requested permission to retire to his dressing-room and make ready to accompany them. Two policemen were accordingly sent with him to the room beyond. Begging them to be seated, Confalonieri hastily stepped behind a curtain, and grasping a ladder concealed there, ascended through a trapdoor to the floor above. Closing the aperture behind him, he fled along a secret passage to a grating giving access to the roof, whence he could readily reach a place of safety in the adjoining buildings. Whether by treachery or an oversight, the grating was firmly fastened and the key missing. Bleeding profusely from the frantic efforts he made to wrench the grating from its hinges, the unfortunate fugitive was dragged out and lodged within the walls of the city prison.

Our heroine, between whom and Confalonieri there was no love lost, relates a characteristic incident which took place barely a month before the count's arrest, and which testifies to his careless contempt of the dangers of the situation. Confalonieri had invited several friends to dine at his villa on Lake Como on October 15, 1821. The guests arrived to find everything in readiness, but no trace of host or hostess. Several hours later these appeared, returning along the road on foot. The count then explained that, being so near the Swiss frontier, he often took advantage of the facility with which he was allowed to cross and recross the boundary to evade the Customs. On this occasion, the fraud had been detected, and his carriage with its contraband contents confiscated.

More fortunate than many of his colleagues of the *Federazione*, the Marquis d'Aragona escaped conviction. The great trial, undoubtedly one of the most important factors in the genesis of the political liberation of Italy, extended over a period of more than two years. Both the Austrian Emperor and Prince Metternich personally investigated the most minute details of the proceedings, for it was early appreciated that social and dynastic issues vital not only to the integrity of the Austrian Empire but to the reconstructed political *régimes* of half Europe were at stake.

It is well-nigh impossible to conceive the anguish of suspense endured by the family of young d'Aragona during the unfolding of the evidence at the trial. Although, owing to the prompt action of his wife, tangible proof of his guilt had been destroyed, yet the *marquis* was well aware that an incautious word, a careless hint, wrung from one of his late associates might be sufficient to entangle him beyond possibility of escape. All Europe shuddered at the refinement of cruelty meted out to the victims which the double-headed eagle of Austria held between its talons. Each day brought details of arrests, convictions, and executions.

Finally, towards the end of 1823, sentence was passed. Alessandro d'Aragona, whom it had been found impossible to convict, owing to the loyalty of his friends and the absence of material proof, was liberated. His colleagues, Confalonieri, Pallavicino, Castiglia, and several others, received the full measure of the law, being condemned to death. For twenty-three days these miserable victims lay under the awful sentence. On the evening of January 12, 1824, news reached Milan that by the clemency of the Emperor the penalty was commuted, the prisoners receiving varying sentences ranging from perpetual to twenty and ten years' confinement in the grim Moravian fortress of Spielberg.

Once more the heavy hand of the Teuton despot clutched the

threads of Italian social life. The darkness of intellectual repression brooded over the land. Milan was the charnel-house of ambition. For the nonce the spirit of independence was cowed. But the latent forces struggling towards the light could no more be artificially repressed than can the fires of Vesuvius. Despite the futility of unorganised agitation, headstrong fanatics, burning for the crown of martyrdom, filled the prisons of Lombardy and Venetia. "The shallows murmur but the depths are dumb."

Thinking men were content to confine themselves to the patient preparation of their countrymen for a political emancipation which they realised could only be achieved with the development of a National Conscience. Planted and fostered by the genius of Berchet, Balbo, Giusti, Niccolini, and a score of lesser lights, this National Ideal gradually took root in the soil, fertilised by the blood of nameless heroes and obscure martyrs, whose cry for freedom was stifled in dank dungeons, or cut short by the executioner's noose. Yet all the while the subtle essence, which the passionate enthusiasm of Joseph Mazzini was to scatter broadcast over the land, was being distilled in those same Austrian prisons of Lombardy and Venetia, or wrung from the souls of the countless exiles who eked out a miserable and precarious existence on a foreign soil.

CHAPTER 2

Marriage of Christina Trivulzio

Within a twelvemonth of the release of her stepfather, Christina Trivulzio was given in marriage to her fellow-townsman, the young Prince Emilio Belgiojoso.

The bride had but recently attained her sixteenth year when, on September 15, 1824, she was led to the altar by this brilliant young patrician, himself but twenty-four. Rich, extremely handsome, amiable and accomplished, and moreover the possessor of a glorious voice, which he used with consummate art, Emilio Belgiojoso was the idol of Milanese salons and of the artistic circles he assiduously frequented.

On her side his wife brought fortune, great beauty, intellectual qualities of the highest order, combined with an extraordinarily arresting charm of person. Yet the union was essentially ill-assorted. Chivalrous and kind, but pleasure-loving and selfish, Don Emilio lacked the steadier qualities which alone could give him any moral ascendency over a nature in which abnormal psychological peculiarities were intensified by distressing pathological disturbances—the princess was subject to epilepsy.

Although she had devoured Voltaire's *Candide* before she was sixteen, the mere sensuality of Donna Christina's complex nature was speedily absorbed by the constant demands of her intellectual appetites, which far outran the cravings of the former. Both husband and wife, differing widely in ideals as well as essentials, were actuated by the strongest passions, and although sympathy continued between them, love fled within a few months of their marriage. Gradually each resumed an independence they were by character and circumstance ill-fitted to sacrifice.

Hardly more than a child in years yet already invested with the pathetic and dangerous glamour attaching to matrimonial disaster, and showing under the hauteur of her delicately cut pale face the tense lines of tragedy, Christina Belgiojoso took her life into her own keeping.

A warm friend of Giovanni Berchet, the poet whose soul-stirring verses fired the heroism of his generation, Emilio Belgiojoso was aroused by him from self-indulgent pleasures to occasional spurts of patriotic fervour. A Carbonaro, although a lukewarm conspirator, the prince later became a disciple and intimate of Mazzini, who, while he deplored his vacillating enthusiasm and frequent lapses from grace, yet recognised his brilliant qualifications and made use of them on occasion. This was ground upon which Donna Christina could follow, nay, outstrip, her fickle spouse. Apart from music, conspiracy was the only interest they had in common, and indeed for many years constituted the basis of their mutual intercourse.

Despite the experiences and warnings of her early youth, the princess yearned to mingle with the patriots who found in political intrigue a semblance of the liberties a stern reality denied them. For a time, the restless energies of our heroine found congenial diversion among the *giardiniere*, as the female adherents of the Carbonaria were euphemistically styled. Under the personal instruction of that arch-conspirator Bianca Milesi, (Bianca Milesi, *Lombardo*, Florence 1905), the young patrician was initiated into the mysteries of sign-manual, passwords, and other occult accessories of a fully equipped secret society.

Manzoni's school of Romanticism, narrow and individualistic in its essentials, had outlived its usefulness, although as a nexus between the old and new philosophies of Italian social and political regeneration it continued to exert a mild influence. The Carbonari, on the other hand, while they supplied the sterner militant qualities in which Manzoni's somewhat bloodless philosophy was lacking, were beginning to lose their hold over national enthusiasm, owing to an increasing cosmopolitanism at once distasteful and incomprehensible to the masses. Plebeian as was its name, the Carbonaria was aristocratic rather than democratic in its aim.

Republicanism found little favour with the bulk of its members, the goal of whose revolutionary propaganda was the supplanting of the despotism of Austria and the autocracy of the Neapolitan Bourbons by a national constitutional monarchy with an Italian prince on the throne of a confederated Italy. The programme was satisfactory, so far as it went, but the organisation was effete. The necessity for new

ALESSANDRO MANZONI.

ambitions, new ideals, which should arouse the lagging enthusiasm of the masses was discerned by Mazzini.

Unlike the Carbonaria he exhorted his followers to place no faith in princes, for whom his scheme of political regeneration and national independence provided no part. His society, "Young Italy," destined to replace the older sect, has been described as a creed and an apostolate rather than a political party. He offered his countrymen a national religion which was to eradicate the social and political evils endured by a downtrodden populace and raise an ideal State on the ruins of thrones and obsolete distinctions of class. Like most visionaries, he aimed too high and overshot the mark.

But the transcendentalism of such a creed dazzled the eclectic intellectuality, while giving vent to the suppressed physical energies of his aristocratic Milanese disciples; although its sociological doctrines could never penetrate the cuirass of their hereditary egotism. Yet if Belgiojoso and his wife subscribed with mental reservations to the republicanism of Mazzini's creed, they nevertheless opened their purse very generously for the advancement of his Utopian schemes for the destruction of tyrannical rule in Italy.

With the cooling of her marital relations the Princess Belgiojoso plunged ever deeper in the treacherous abyss of conspiracy. Vanity, lack of occupation, undoubtedly contributed to her early enthusiasms, but a very sincere and passionate patriotism was the outgrowth of such meaner incentives. As was to be expected, the mysterious associations and frequent absences of so prominent a social personality did not escape the lynx-eyed Milanese police. Her political antecedents, or rather those of her family, as well as her incipient personal reputation as a dabbler in subversive doctrines, marked her in Vienna as hostile to the Austrian *régime*, and as such one to be carefully watched.

From Geneva, where in 1830 the princess for some months followed a treatment for her nervous disorder, ever-present spies kept the home authorities minutely informed of her mode of life and the elements of the society she frequented. The comings and goings of her great travelling coach with its load of cumbersome luggage, the routes followed and the stops made, all is accurately chronicled and preserved in the Secret Archives of the Lombard-Venetian Government deposited in Milan. No action of hers at this period would seem to have been deemed too trivial to warrant the transmission of a detailed report to Milan.

Even the peregrinations of her *major-domo* on errands connected

GIUSEPPE MAZZINI

with his mistress's private affairs appear to have possessed mysterious importance. Under date of October 21, 1830, (Case cxxviii. Secret Archives, Milan), the tireless scribe who dogged her steps complains of the eccentricities which mark the progress of the erratic princess it is his duty to "shadow." Particularly does he censure her conduct at Lugano, where on her arrival she loses no time in issuing invitations for a magnificent ball, filling her *salons* with a heterogeneous crowd, among which are many political exiles who have sought safety on the hospitable soil of the Swiss Confederation.

The brilliancy of this sumptuous entertainment, obviously a bid for popularity with the subversive political element, gave great umbrage at Vienna. The astute Metternich, in the philosophy of whose statecraft detail played so important a part, recognised the dangerous firebrand this beautiful and intriguing aristocrat—his sworn and implacable personal enemy—might become if allowed to indulge unchecked her taste for political heresy. Through the intermediary of Count Hartig, governor of Lombardy-Venetia, Metternich sought to coerce the princess to return to Milan, where the vigilance of his police could more effectually frustrate conspiracy.

By special messenger the intimation was conveyed to her that her prolonged sojourn in Switzerland was illegal from the fact of her having neglected to apply for the requisite papers, and that an immediate return to her native city was desirable. Flourishing in the face of the astonished official an unlimited passport issued by the Austrian Ambassador in Florence, and countersigned by his colleague at Berne, the triumphant princess pressed upon his notice the disconcerting fact that, in addition to this, she held a certificate of Swiss citizenship. This latter document had been granted by the Government of the Canton of Tessin (October, 1830) in accordance with the provision of the decree of 1808, whereby all members of the House of Trivulzio held the right to claim the protection of the Republic.

Baffled in his attempt to control the liberty of his taunting foe, Metternich sought to attain his object through the channels of diplomacy. An intimidating despatch was forwarded to the Tessinese authorities requesting the surrender of those fugitives accused of high treason, and the immediate expulsion of all other political refugees; their presence constituting, it was asserted, a menace to the tranquillity of the bordering provinces under Austrian rule, as well as those of the Kingdom of Sardinia. Failure to comply with these demands would be viewed as an unfriendly act, and the Government of his Imperial and Royal Majesty would be constrained to have recourse to measures—consistent with the rights of nations—calculated to compel the Canton to an adequate observance of existing obligations.

Before such a thinly veiled threat prudence was the better part of valour: yet the Swiss authorities had no intention of belying their traditional reputation for hospitality. Cunningly placating the irritated emperor with the specious sham of a special commission appointed to investigate the imputations, the government continued to afford not only asylum but material aid to such refugees as were manifestly victims of a political tyranny, collusion with which was unthinkable to freeborn men.

Meanwhile the popularity of the princess with the good Republicans of Lugano was steadily increasing. The glamour of her aristocratic birth artfully blended with the charm of an unaffectedly democratic bearing; her well-known devotion to the sacred tenets of Liberalism, together with the attractive flavour of heroism due to her haughty defiance of the Austrian Government; all went towards assuring her an exceptional position in the good graces of officials and populace alike. Moreover, her charity—indiscriminating as her hospitality—was boundless, and lavished impartially upon the dispirited exile, to whom she appeared as a very goddess of Liberty, and the local indigent, for the relief of whose humble wants her purse-strings were ever loosened.

Recognising the strength of her present position, the Austrian spy detailed to watch the movements of this troublesome conspirator reported to his chief that it would be unwise to urge too persistently the expulsion of so popular a person.

So, Donna Christina sojourned peacefully and uneventfully with her Swiss hosts until the inherent unrest peculiar to her temperament drove her to pastures new and the dangerous distractions of conspiracy on Italian soil. She decided on a visit to Genoa, the turbulent and disaffected seaport of Piedmont, where conspiracy was rife, and where she was soon actively engaged in furthering the audacious schemes of the Liberals.

The journey from Lugano had been achieved without hindrance, thanks to a passport, dated in that town on October 5, 1830, wherein the adventurous holder was described as a native of Switzerland. How the document was procured remains a mystery. Correspondence between the Governor of Lombardy and the Austrian diplomatic representative at Berne waxed acrid over the incident; but the recalcitrant princess only laughed in her sleeve over the official embroilment her movements created. Matters became more serious, however, when tidings of her reprehensible conduct in Genoa reached Milan. The spy, who was never far distant, lost little time in reporting to his superiors the character of the company she frequented. The princess herself was careless of concealment, giving vent to expression of her political antipathies with a recklessness which caused her companions to tremble.

Again, Count Hartig set the machinery of diplomacy in motion, calling upon the Austrian Minister at Turin to secure at all costs the detention of his tormentor. At this time Piedmont still groaned under the reactionary rule of Charles Felix, and a hint from Vienna was tantamount to a command. The Genoese police actually received orders to arrest the princess; but she had been warned, and, with the aid of her friend Bianca Milesi, she donned a disguise and escaped by a back entrance. Embarking on a vessel bound for Leghorn, accompanied by her maid, Donna Christina's objective point was France. Details of this hasty flight were later extracted from the princess's maid, Maria Longoni, by the Austrian police, (State Archives in Milan, *Atti della Polizia*, ii. 5669. *Protocollo Segreto*. According to Maria Longoni the princess embarked at Genoa for Marseilles direct.); but there is good reason for the belief that the woman's account is inaccurate.

La Cecilia saw the princess in Leghorn, where she awaited an opportunity of escaping to Marseilles. Her presence in Leghorn was made known to him by a fellow-conspirator, Baron Poerio, who wrote:

> You will make the acquaintance of one of the most beautiful and charming women in Italy. Persecuted by Austria, she seeks an asylum in revolutionary France: there with her name and her talents she can be of the greatest service to the Italian cause. See her at once: the enclosed card will make you known to her. Through her the Committee at Leghorn will establish communications with the patriots of France.—*Memorie di La Cecilia*, vol. i.

Fascinated in his turn, the Neapolitan conspirator was for many years closely associated with the fair revolutionist, who "with an imposing personality and perfection of form united learning and genius."

The sojourn at Leghorn was a short one, and in due course Marseilles was safely reached. But even here her every movement was watched and chronicled by one Pietro Svegliati, a spy in the pay of the Austrian authorities, who addressed his letters to Giovanni Candiani,

Poste Restante, Milan. Both names are probably fictitious, but the voluminous correspondence of this indefatigable scribe, preserved in the Secret Archives at the Palazzo Elvetico in Milan, is official.

Under date of February 26, 1831, Svegliati informs his employer that the Princess Belgiojoso is living in strict seclusion with young Bolognini, of Reggio.

> She relates, that the Government of Milan has sequestered all her property in order to constrain her to return home, whither, however, she has decided not to set foot until freed from its oppressors.—Case cxlii.

A month later the estimable Pietro advises his friend in Milan that the princess is deeply in love with young Bolognini, and that she receives much company in Marseilles.

> Her house is a veritable club, and the rendezvous of hosts of Liberals.

Svegliati professes to be accurately informed of all that passes within the four walls of her apartment, and every three or four days the post is burdened with long dissertations, the material for which would appear to have been collected round the tables of the Café Americano. Copies, or extracts, from many of his letters were sent to Turin; which would go to prove that both the Lombard and Piedmontese authorities attached considerable importance to the news they contained.

While in Marseilles Christina Belgiojoso had become intimately associated with the new school of patriots founded by Mazzini.

The collapse of the Carbonari insurrection against the tyranny of pope and princes (Feb. 1831) disposed the minds of Italian patriots towards the new philosophy preached by the young Genoese enthusiast. Henceforth the society he founded, and which he called "Young Italy," became the focus of Nationalism. The rules of this association excluded from membership (except in special cases) all persons over forty years of age, for Mazzini pinned his faith on the men and women of his own generation. They alone, he believed, were capable of throwing off prejudice: from them alone could he expect the high enthusiasm and abnegation the social and political redemption of their country demanded. The Carbonaro chiefs he considered had failed because their revolutionary programme and its antiquated theories were no longer in sympathy with the ideals of the younger generation of patriots. The Carbonari had held aloft the constitutional monarchy as the goal of revolutionary reform: "Young Italy" declared itself frankly republican.

A moment of wavering doubt, perhaps of hope, Mazzini had certainly entertained when Prince Charles Albert succeeded in Piedmont the reactionary Charles Felix, who, after tormenting his subjects for ten years, died in April, 1831. Even the stern, uncompromising founder of "Young Italy" had not entirely escaped the glamour attaching to the strange personality of the quondam Liberal, the fickle dispenser of the ephemeral constitution of 1821.

To the new king, Mazzini addressed an open letter calling upon him to place himself at the head of the Nationalists, to wage war on Austria and on the foreign princelings who usurped the thrones of Tuscany, Parma, Modena, and Lucca. But Charles Albert had been made to pay too dearly for the ambitions and enthusiasms of his youth; and the harsh discipline to which he had afterwards been subjected, instead of strengthening his character, had merely intensified his cunning.

Ambitious in a half-hearted, hesitating way, he totally lacked both the initiative and persistence indispensable in the leader of a national cause. "Half-friar, half Knight," Charles Albert mortified the flesh with fasting and the wearing of a hair-shirt, and cringed before the admonitions of his Jesuit confessor. The clerical influences which ruled his political conscience moulded his judgment and played upon his inherent mysticism. He was easily persuaded that the political unity of the Italian Peninsula and the social enfranchisement such union of necessity entailed constituted a menace to Throne and Church.

For centuries the Papal policy had been opposed to the union or confederation of Italy, even under the rule of Rome, for it fully appreciated that the Guelf movement undertaken in its behalf must in the end belittle, or even destroy, the power of the Church in the Peninsula. The Papacy foresaw that the young Nation, once united, must inevitably escape from the tutelage of Rome, even were the head of the Church likewise the recognised political head of the Nation, and this by virtue of the truism that one form perishes when another replaces it. The frequent foreign invasions of Italy were often encouraged by the Popes as a wholesome restraint on the threatened independence of popular movements. The Papacy itself had little to fear from such invasions, which generally stopped short at the doors of the Vatican, cringing before the threat of excommunication.

For reasons such as these a political confederation of the Italian

States betook, in the eyes of the clericals, of the nature of a calamity. Hence the preservation of Austrian influence—predominant throughout the Peninsula—constituted the most efficient guarantee for the continued prestige of the Roman Church, which obviously had nothing to gain, and possibly much to lose, through the vulgarisation of the principle of nationality. The soundness of this argument was to be amply proved in the case of Pius IX., whose partial application of the Liberal and Nationalist principles he had imbibed during his cardinalate resulted in the temporary wreck of his pontificate, the restoration of his temporal power being due to foreign intervention alone.

To Christina Belgiojoso, as to many another expectant patriot languishing in exile, the news of the accession of Charles Albert came as the promise of an era of Constitutionalism for Piedmont. The advent to power of the erstwhile Liberal must surely signify the entrance of the thin end of the wedge which should force open the dark recesses of Absolutism throughout Italy. Despite the failure of the recent Carbonaro movement, which had founded its hopes of success on the revolution in France of the previous July, Italian exiles in Paris still believed in the assurances given by Louis Philippe's ministers that Italy might look to France for efficacious support, at least in so far as the principle of non-intervention was concerned.

This was construed as meaning that Austria would be warned that interference with the domestic affairs of independent Italian States would no longer be tolerated. Such an intimation, it was felt, must foreshadow the spread of representative institutions in those States where the arrogant meddling of Austria was an abomination to prince and people alike, and ultimately sound the knell of Austrian domination in the Italian provinces under her political control. Alas! Charles Albert's accession proved not the overture of a new era, but the epilogue of the old one. Instead of seizing the opportunity, and backed by France, proclaiming constitutional liberties in Piedmont, the king scornfully rejected Mazzini's appeal, and began a cruel persecution and relentless repression of the Liberals within his dominions.

It may be said that the opening years of the reign of Charles Albert surpassed in ferocity, perhaps, even the enormities perpetrated in Naples and the States of the Church. Ecclesiastical, as well as civil, judicial procedure hounded the social and political reformer to his doom, the double censorship of the secret tribunals—lay and clerical—leaving no loophole for escape. Yet, incomprehensible as it must appear, the vision of Piedmont leading Italy in the path of administrative and so-

Pius IX

cial liberties—even in a war of national emancipation lingered in the minds of many who now groaned under the despotic intolerance of the man they were still eager to proclaim their saviour.

During all these dark years of Jesuit supremacy Italian Liberals in the concrete remained steadfast to the conviction that their chosen leader would overcome his "craven fear of being great," free himself from the shameful bondage of foreign and ecclesiastical suggestion, and reveal himself in all sincerity the champion of the National Cause. Nor was their faith wholly misplaced, although years of anguish and illusion were to intervene before their hero—a sorry travesty of an heroic ideal—tentatively laid the corner-stone upon which the temple of Italian Liberty was to be built, strong and enduring, by his son, Victor Emmanuel II.

CHAPTER 3

Her life in Paris

In his letter of April 9, 1831, Pietro Svegliati notifies his correspondent in Milan that the Princess Belgiojoso shook the dust of Marseilles from her feet on the preceding Tuesday, he adds:

> The sojourn at Marseilles must have cost her a great deal of money, many youths profited by her expenditure, taking advantage of her generous patriotism, and at the same time casting a slur on her reputation and proclaiming her a Messalina.

That the singular independence of her life and character gave rise to all manner of dastardly imputations is hardly to be wondered at, but it must be borne in mind that it was to the personal advantage of this salaried spy to paint his victim in as dark colours as possible.

Paris was at that time the Mecca of the revolutionary exile; and to Paris the princess incontinently repaired.

Meanwhile, Prince Metternich, baulked of his prey, sought to bring the haughty Milanese to terms by the confiscation of her property. A decree was published in Milan announcing that unless the Princess Christina Belgiojoso-Trivulzio returned to the States of his Imperial Royal and Apostolic Majesty within three months, and presented herself before the Provincial Delegation, she would be declared civilly dead and her property confiscated. Simultaneously with the issue of the above decree all sources of revenue under Austrian jurisdiction were sequestrated.

This arbitrary proceeding proved as ineffectual as previous threats: the high-spirited woman with whom the emperor had to deal would have died of starvation in a garret rather than bow to a tyranny which sought to constrain her personal liberty.

Her emotional fires unquenched despite physical ailments and worries over the possible material consequences of the decree of confiscation, the princess threw herself heart and soul into the schemes which the impulsiveness of Mazzini devised for the liberation of Italy. Her soul ran riot amidst the mysticism of the poet-agitator's ideals, and although her eminently practical intelligence found, perhaps, meagre satisfaction in the results achieved, yet her love of action was constantly appealed to by the romantic daring of the enterprises attempted.

Life in Paris during the earlier period of her exile provided ample scope for the somewhat theatrical indulgence in eccentric contrast which she delighted in. Although her income was greatly reduced while the decree sequestrating her property was in force, the princess was never allowed to want, generous provision being surreptitiously made by her wealthy relations. There exist, however, ugly rumours that at this period the princess weakened in her anti-Austrian defiance, and addressed humble protests, approaching dangerously the form of supplications, to the Austrian Ambassador in Paris, Count Appony, concerning her financial straits.

In these letters, she is accused of obsequiously professing herself "*Aux ordres du gouvernement de mon pays*," while attempting explanations of her recent conduct. (Alessandro Luzio, *Corriere della Sera*, Milan, August 3-4, 1902.) That she had her moments of weakness is more than probable: that she made some form of protest against the arbitrary confiscation of her income is also conceivable; but there would appear to exist no irrefutable evidence that she humbled herself before her enemy. On the contrary, her contemporaries are rather inclined to blame her stiff-necked independence, although they scoff at the "pose" which sought to produce the semblance of poverty.

Nevertheless, it suited her present purpose to make the most out of the political martyrdom to which she was subjected, and to show up Austrian vengeance against a defenceless woman in the most lurid hues. Legend has it that over the door of the squalid apartment she secured on the top floor of a modest house in a poor neighbourhood she caused to be placed this inscription: *La Princesse Malheureuse* a far-fetched play of words on the meaning of her married name.

Be this as it may, the princess neglected no opportunity of impressing upon her acquaintance and the general public the incongruity of her present position. Ostentatiously she painted fans and glass for a livelihood, invariably informing purchasers that it was owing to the harsh cruelty of the Austrian usurper that she was reduced to such

ADOLPHE THIERS

straits.

Among the visitors who climbed the long flights of her dingy stairs was Adolphe Thiers, whose admiration for the beautiful exile amounted to passion. Again, the voice of rumour has it that when the future President of the French Republic accepted an invitation to share the scant fare of his fascinating hostess he was wont himself to do the cooking, and that his skill in the preparation of an omelette was enthusiastically welcomed. The astute princess did not, however, make use of Monsieur Thiers's culinary talents alone. At her instigation, the public utterances of the French statesman were often impregnated with a pro-Italianism which gave serious umbrage to Metternich and the Governor of the Italian provinces under Austrian rule.

Through the influence of her infatuated admirer, Princess Belgio-joso was accorded a hearing under the roof of the French Chamber of Deputies, and before a select audience she made an eloquent and stirring appeal to the sister-nation for aid to her countrymen in their struggle for political regeneration. (R. Barbiera, *La Principessa Belgio-joso*.) The incongruity of this semi-official tolerance of a profession of subversive theories, at a moment when Mazzini was under the ban of expulsion by the French Government for similar offences, is highly significant of the extent of the fascination exercised over Thiers and his associates by the Italian princess.

The crisis of the Revolution of July had not yet been dissipated. The Monarchy still lacked the force and prestige of stability, and all danger of a relapse into the revolutionary era so lately ended was by no means over. Europe was as yet uncertain whether Louis Philippe's accession meant peace, or whether his government would be drawn into the vortex of international politics, at the risk of provoking a coalition of the Conservative Cabinets, and war. The Republicanism of Thiers was of later growth; at this period, he had loyally joined is-sues with the Constitutional Monarchy which owed its being to the Revolution of July (1830). (C. de Mazade, *Monsieur Thiers*.) Few were in a better position to appreciate the perils which might result from foreign complications during the critical stages of the consolidation of the new *régime*. Yet this hot-headed young statesman of thirty-four practically risked not only his personal political future, but the prestige of his country, for the smiles of his enchantress, who was also the all-powerful Metternich's bitterest foe.

If the portraits by Vidal and Lehmann are faithful, there is small wonder that Paris went mad over the Italian beauty. Especially in the picture by Lehmann are the remarkable characteristics of the face apparent. The princess is represented sitting with clasped hands, gazing directly at the spectator. The smooth dark hair, parted in the middle, is carried back, covering the ears, only the extremity of the lobes, with two large pearls attached, being visible; the great lustrous black eyes burning under a high forehead, and set in a perfect oval, the colouring of which is like wax or old marble; the delicate lines of nose and mouth; the long, slim neck, springing from shoulders almost too frail to support the small, well-shaped head; all go to complete a face in which there is no trace of sensuality, but from which, on the contrary, radiates the spirituality of the ascetic. Contemporaneous descriptions dwell upon the deathlike pallor of the complexion, on the excessive frailty and languor of her person, and assert that all the physical and intellectual vitality of the princess appeared concentrated in those wonderful eyes.

Older heads than Thiers's were turned by the indescribable charm of manner and person possessed by Christina Belgiojoso. Among her victims she numbered the veteran General La Fayette, the friend and companion of Washington. (Beaumont-Vassy, *Les Salons de Paris*.) The old Revolutionary hero sympathised understandingly with her aspirations for the independence of her beloved Italy, and was ever ready with aid and counsel. Purely platonic as was the admiration of the distinguished patriarch, his devotion was unlimited. The most assiduous of her visitors at a time when financial embarrassments, or the pretence of such, kept many from her door, his efforts to serve her were not confined to politics, for he sought with the weight of his personal influence to effect a reconciliation between her and her husband.

Although the estrangement was at this time complete, no bitterness existed, the separation being the outcome of mutual convenience. The conspicuous eccentricity of Christina's mode of life inevitably gave rise to scandal; but, as has been said, it is questionable whether the insinuations of the agents of the Austrian Government were not inspired by personal interest. The detailed accusations contained in the reports jealously preserved among the Secret Archives of the Lombard-Venetian Government at Milan are unconvincing and often contradictory. Her every action was chronicled by persistent spies, and it is conceivable that these rivalled one another in their efforts to procure sensational "copy" for their employers.

From one of these secret agents, writing under date of October 25, 1831, we learn that while the princess hardly ever went to a theatre,

La Fayette

she, on the other hand, never missed a session of the Chamber of Deputies, and that she attended regularly the meetings of the followers of Saint-Simon. The system of philosophy elaborated by this social and religious reformer appealed forcibly to the princess, who found in its intellectual communism and admission of the equality of the sexes in all the relations of life substantial recognition of her own social ideals.

As Austria at that period discouraged the intellectual emancipation of her Italian subjects even more energetically than Russia deals with the advanced ideals of Tolstoi today, the heretical theories of Saint-Simonism immeasurably shocked official susceptibilities in Vienna and Milan. Temperamentally an eclectic and a faddist, Princess Christina's militant connection with the Utopian schemes of the disciples of the celebrated French *marquis* was of short duration. A thousand interests claimed her time and filled the cells of her peculiarly receptive brain. Shortly after her arrival in Paris we hear of her founding classes for young girls, and herself instructing her *protégées* in drawing, music, and embroidery.

Whether the politics, philosophy, and philanthropy which crowded the hours and fed tireless intellectual activities excluded sentiments of a more tender and personal nature it is hazardous to affirm. In his correspondence, the aforementioned spy hints unequivocally at the significance to be attached to the presence of a young man—Bolognini by name—who followed the princess from Marseilles, and without whom she was rarely seen abroad. This disdainful scorn of conventionalities inevitably exposed the beautiful exile to scandalous gossip, and as we proceed with her career we shall find many episodes over which her biographer must draw a veil, both from a laudable desire to screen the reputation of his heroine, and because of conflicting testimony.

Most of her contemporaries concur, however, in believing her temperamentally immune where temptations which must have wrecked a more sensual nature are concerned. Moreover, General La Fayette's faith in his ability to effect a reconciliation with her husband would seem to indicate that in this instance Christina's apparent encouragement of an amorous swain was founded on a purely utilitarian basis. (La Cecilia, *Memorie*, vol. i.)

La Fayette was, however, perhaps not aware of the manner in which Prince Emilio Belgiojoso was consoling himself during the estrangement from his truant spouse. The same secret correspondence furnishes a picture of the handsome prince at the feet of the famous

Countess Guiccioli, Lord Byron's ex-*innamorata*, at this time tempo-rarily residing at Geneva. When the Guiccioli came to Paris she was closely followed by her devoted admirer, and, accompanied by her second husband, the Marquis de Boissy, occasionally appeared at Ma-dame de Belgiojoso's receptions. The old *marquis* is reported to have been inordinately proud of the former relations of his still beautiful wife with the immortal bard. Gossip relates that he once presented her to Louis Philippe in the following terms:

> The Marquise de Boissy, my wife, formerly the mistress of Lord Byron.

Lady Blessington, who had known both Byron and the Guiccioli at Genoa in 1824, was also a frequent visitor at the Belgiojoso resi-dence, and contributed vastly to the entertainment of her malicious hostess with her witty reminiscences of the childish jealousies of the fair countess when "*her*" poet cast soft glances in any other direction.

During the opening years of the reign of Louis Philippe, Paris was a seething cauldron of political unrest. France was already disappoint-ed in her Citizen King; while Legitimist Europe, frankly distrustful, recoiled from the principles of the July Revolution, and held aloof. It was the reign of the *bourgeosie*; synonymous in France with mediocrity. Court, Administration, Army—all was *bourgeois*. Moreover, the undig-nified bids for popularity made by the king excited the derision of his subjects, while his transparent insincerity aroused their suspicion. La Fayette had been in good faith, nevertheless, when he promised France "that best of Republics, a loyal king."

Although the veteran general had lost much of his popularity, and had been deprived by a vote of the Chamber of the supreme com-mand of the National Guard, he yet preserved an immense influ-ence over the government. His magnificently decorated *salons* were continually thronged with French and foreign visitors of all sorts and conditions. Generals and deputies elbowed dukes and smug bourgeois exulting in the triumph of their mediocrity; journalists and artistic celebrities foregathered with bankers and financial agents of every standing. A large proportion of the attendance was formed by political exiles and emigrants from all countries, so that the bewildered novice found himself surrounded by a babel of conversation in most of the living languages of Europe.

Amidst this heterogeneous assemblage the old general slowly wan-dered, distributing affable greetings and conventional courtesies, together with words of encouragement and hope to the exiles, and in some instances, promises in the name of the government. (La Cecilia, *op. cit.* vol. iii) His sympathies with the Italian Liberals and their aspirations for constitutional government were genuine. To his influence was attributed the inaction of the French authorities while preparations were in progress for the invasion of Savoy by a horde of Italian insurrectionists—an undertaking which the fall of the Lafitte Cabinet, and the advent to power of Casimir Périer, nipped in the bud.

One hundred thousand *francs* had been subscribed towards this scheme by the Princess Belgiojoso, (Luzio thinks the sum should be reduced by one-half), who parted with her jewels in order to raise the funds. On learning of her sacrifice, Emilio Belgiojoso wrote offering forty thousand *francs* towards replenishing her jewel case. This proposition the princess gently declined, with a dignity we cannot but admire. In her letter of thanks to her estranged husband the writer dwells on the fact that she is at present in too great financial straits to allow herself the luxury of jewels, and that had she the sum he mentions at her disposal she would prefer employing it to meet some of her more pressing obligations.

The letter closes with a personal reference which affords an inkling of the psychological maze in which the exiled and lonely woman wandered:

> It is perhaps true that physical health can often replace spiritual wellbeing: I have experienced both simultaneously; but at the same moment I lost both: hence I cannot judge which of the two would best console me for the loss of the other.—From letter in the collection of Signer Vanbianchi, cited by Barbiera.

Involved and enigmatic as the sentence is, there is distinctly discernible that profound disillusionment, that physical and mental lassitude, which, in spite of periodical prodigious intellectual activity, remains the key-note of a character replete with contradictions.

It is difficult to unravel the threads which lent a plausible guarantee of success to the seemingly desperate undertaking which enlisted the princess's sympathy. The object of the expedition was to bring Charles Albert to terms; and the conspirators would appear to have had an understanding with their French colleagues by virtue of which France was to receive Savoy in exchange for the island of Corsica. La Cecilia prints the text of a diplomatic convention, signed in Paris on February 18, 1831, by the Marquis La Fayette and the members of the Insurrectionary Committee, containing, in a preamble and three articles, the specific conditions under which, following a successful issue of the raid, solemn ratifications shall be exchanged. (La Cecilia, *Memorie*, vol. i.)

A force of some sixteen hundred volunteers assembled at Lyons, and actually began their march southwards, but were overtaken, turned back, and disbanded on the receipt of imperative orders from Paris. The duplicity of Louis Philippe seemed apparent. By Italians he was bitterly denounced for attempting to curry favour with Austria by encouraging with intent to betray the confidence of the conspirators. Perhaps, however, the resolute stand taken by Prince Metternich in refusing to recognise the principle of non-intervention proclaimed by France, and his announcement to the French Ambassador at Vienna that Austrian troops would in every instance relentlessly stamp out revolutionary movements in Italy, even at the risk of war, had something to do with Louis Philippe's change of face.

The blow staggered the Italian patriots who had looked to France for connivance if not open aid. La Fayette was included in the opprobrium heaped upon the government, although it was soon manifest that the sanguine but not always perspicacious old hero had been as much the dupe of the canny monarch as his fellow-conspirators. Perhaps the king welcomed the opportunity to discredit the general. "If I cannot emancipate myself from the tutelage of La Fayette," had been his lament on more than one occasion, "I must ever remain a king *in partibus*."

The beautiful Italian princess had been a frequent and honoured guest at the house of La Fayette—disdainfully styled by the Legitimists "the caravansary of revolutionary Europe." As was to be expected, the most insignificant utterances of the grand old man who had figured so conspicuously in the Revolutions of America and France, and who had practically decided the form of government to be adopted after that of 1830, were listened to with bated breath by the reverential circle which constantly surrounded him. All others paled before the venerated patriarch, and although the personality of the Princess Belgiojoso was not one to pass unnoticed even in such a presence, she found herself disagreeably overshadowed, when not actually relegated to the inner circle where the women of the family held less brilliant court.

To a temperament such as hers this was simply intolerable. Like Louis Philippe, she chafed under the tutelage of her too-distinguished friend, and declined to subject herself to the humiliation of playing second fiddle before an audience with which she craved the place of honour. Pride of race and pride of intellect demanded the formation of a court of her own where she might reign supreme in uncontested sovereignty. This the ambitious social and political Revolutionist now proceeded to inaugurate in close proximity to the stronghold of her venerated rival.

The various Italian clubs founded by refugees in Paris were one and all characterised by the looseness of the restrictions governing admission. Little care being taken to sift the evidences of good faith, thieves, swindlers, and spies masqueraded under the guise of patriotism. Men and women of all social grades and every political creed— or heresy—discussed at random the maddest enterprises and the most Utopian theories. By the would-be State-builders the throne of an Italian kingdom still unborn, or the presidential chair of an equally embryonic republic or federation, was variously disposed of at each successive meeting.

Although Christina Belgiojoso, like Mazzini, was at this period an advocate of agitation at any cost, she could but recognise the sterility of such vapourings. During these years (1831-34) her own ambitions rarely soared beyond the expulsion of Austria from Northern Italy, and the proclamation of constitutional liberties. Democratic as were her political aspirations, and dearly as she loved notoriety and the evidences of popular adulation, her instinctive fastidiousness revolted against the claims of Demagogism. On the other hand, she rejected the arrogant pretensions of an oft lean-witted aristocracy to social or political pre-eminence. Thus, while rightly despising mediocrity in any form, she arbitrarily based her political standards on a personal eclecticism dangerously akin to intolerance. Again, while she totally lacked the broad-mindedness inseparable from true statesmanship she was, nevertheless, abundantly possessed of the intuitive acumen of the politician.

It is a well-nigh hopeless task to successfully probe the hidden workings of the simplest human souls, and the difficulties are increased a thousand-fold when dealing with a nature as mobile, as complex, as mystical as that of Christina Belgiojoso. Again, and again we ask ourselves, as we unfold her troubled career, how much was real and how much sham in the jumble of fierce enthusiasms and flaunting patriotism so rebelliously proclaimed. Yet we dare not accuse her of insincerity, in spite of manifold inconsistencies and temperamental artificiality. No, we must believe her to have been sincere according to her lights; but we admit that she constantly returned from her pursuit of Truth hand in hand with Paradox, herself serenely unconscious of her error.

CHAPTER 4

Birth of Princess's Daughter

Although originally founded for the propaganda of the political ideals to the furtherance of which she so generously subscribed, the *salon* of the Princess Belgiojoso speedily attracted the intellectual *élite* of the Parisian fashionable world. To the more refined of Italian refugees the promiscuousness of the clubs was distasteful; and these found the drawing-rooms of their noble countrywoman, in which scholarly attainments and social qualifications were accorded due recognition, an inestimable boon.

Meanwhile the accusations of conspiracy to undermine and destroy Austrian rule in the provinces of Lombardy-Venetia brought against the prince and princess were carefully investigated by the special tribunals in Milan. The "political depravity" of the aristocratic couple was severely censured by the secret police. Even amidst the pleasures and dissipations of Paris, where he led a life of fashionable ease, Prince Emilio Belgiojoso was suspected of indulging in reprehensible political heresies, although his patriotic zeal shows but palely when contrasted with that of his uncompromisingly hostile wife. Nevertheless, his friendship with Mazzini was irrefutably proven; his financial co-operation with insurrectionary schemes being known, as well as his connection with "Young Italy," an association which was beginning to arouse the bitterest resentment among the official minions of Absolutism.

Both the prince and princess encouraged and substantially aided Mazzini when, in July, 1833, the agitator repaired to Geneva to organise the new raid he planned upon Savoy. Exactly what it was hoped to accomplish is uncertain, although probably Mazzini sought to regain his prestige, which had suffered owing to the collapse of the military plot in Piedmont, and to clinch his hold over wavering followers by

CHARLES ALBERT, KING OF SARDINIA

forcing an issue, and he may have counted on a small initial success to rekindle the military insurrection which Charles Albert had so savagely repressed. Again, his enthusiasm outran his knowledge of the situation; again the visionary theorist proved his incapacity either as a leader or a judge of men.

The command of the expedition he confided to General Ramorino, a Savoyard soldier of fortune whose sympathy with the cause he was engaged to serve was doubtful, and who squandered a considerable portion of the fund placed at his disposal for the equipment of the raiders. When eventually Ramorino tore himself away from the pleasures of Paris, and placed himself at the head of the rabble of cosmopolitan adventurers who mustered eight hundred strong, and who were causing the Genevan authorities very grave preoccupations, it was only to lead them aimlessly about, and after a few insignificant skirmishes, disband them and recross the frontier.

The part played by the princess in the preparation of this foolhardy fiasco was of course well known in Milan and Vienna, and caused intense irritation in official circles. Yet on July 24, 1833, the proceedings against the prince were suddenly suspended in conformity with a personal order of the Emperor Francis I. On the other hand, Prince Antonio Belgiojoso, a brother of Prince Emilio, was arrested in Turin and thrown into prison, where he languished under imputation of high treason until a special Imperial pardon also set him free.

On the same day which witnessed the inexplicable suspension—in reality, abandonment—of her husband's trial, the criminal tribunal of Milan formally indicted Christina Belgiojoso on a charge of high treason, and decreed her arrest. Again, the Imperial clemency was inexplicably exercised, although indirectly, one delay after another pigeon-holing the proceedings until they were virtually abandoned. (Barbiera, *Principessa Belgiojoso. Secret Archives, Milan, 1134-1161.*) Not so, however, in the cases of her fellow-conspirators, Argenti and Albinola. Condemned to death, their sentences were eventually commuted to eight years in chains in the gruesome Spielberg, followed by deportation to New York.

With the virtual quashing of criminal proceedings against her, the sequestration of her property ceased, and the princess once more came into the enjoyment of her ample income. She now occupied a sumptuous residence in Paris, and she found herself, moreover, enabled to indulge to the full her decidedly eccentric tastes in decoration. Several contemporaries have left descriptions of this fantastic abode which

Théophile Gautier styled "*Uné vraie série de catafalques.*" The walls of the large square drawing-room were hung with a sombre velvet, almost black, upon which silver stars were embroidered. The furniture being upholstered in the same gloomy material, the effect produced when the apartment was lighted with the wax-tapers then in use was startlingly suggestive of a mortuary chamber.

In strong contrast with this funereal apartment followed a bedroom entirely hung and upholstered in white silk, the bed and various furnishings and fittings either being entirely of silver or harmonising in tone with the soft sheen of that metal, and lending an air of vestal purity to the whole. The melodramatic effect was further enhanced by the presence of a turbaned negro, a species of high priest and guardian of the sanctuary, who slept in the ante-chamber, and was continuously on duty by day. Madame d'Agoult (best known in literature by her pseudonym, "Daniel Stern") writes:

> Never did a woman, more fully understand the art of effect than did the Princess Belgiojoso. She searched for and found it in everything: today in the form of a negro and the study of theology; tomorrow in the Arab whom she paraded in her carriage in order to intrigue the frequenters of the Bois. Yesterday she found it in conspiracy, in exile, in the very shells of the eggs of the omelette she herself prepared over her fire at the time it suited her to feign ruin. Pale, thin to emaciation, with eyes of flame, she cultivated the aspect of a spectre or a phantom. Readily also, for the sake of effect, she gave credence to certain rumours which put in her hands the cup and dagger of the Borgia.—Daniel Stern, *Mes Souvenirs,* Paris, 1877.

Of course, the portrait is exaggerated; but it possesses the incisive fidelity of a clever caricature mercilessly exposing the foibles of its victim. Another glimpse of the princess's peculiarities is offered by the same pen, and describes a scene when her theological craze was at its height. Visitors usually "surprised" the princess at her devotions in her private oratory, where, "under the yellow shafts of light falling through Gothic stained glass, between dusty folios, a skull at her feet," she knelt at her *prie-dieu*, lost in meditation.

The visitor had probably crossed in the ante-chamber one of the fashionable preachers of the day—the Abbé Combalot or the Abbé Coeur, whose daily ministrations and counsel aided the fair theologian in the arduous task upon which her intellectual activity was now

Cavour

engaged. It was of this apostle of Christian Democracy that Cavour wrote:

Les doctrines de l'abbé Coeur ont penetré dans mon intelligence et remué mon coeur: le jour où je les verrai sincèrement et généralement adoptées par l'Eglise, je deviendrai probablement un catholique aussi ardent que toi.—Letter to Rossi di Santa Rosa, Epistolario i.

(The doctrines of the Abbe Heart penetrated my mind and stirred my heart: the day when I shall see them sincerely and generally adopted by the Church, I will probably become a Catholic as ardent as you.)

Accustomed as Parisian society was to the astonishing transformations of the distinguished Italian exile, the world of fashion and of intellect stood aghast when, in 1842, the fat volumes of her *Essai sur la formation du dogme catholique* made their appearance. (Only the first two volumes were published in 1842, the two remaining volumes being brought out later.) By her contemporaries it was deemed impossible that she could have personally acquired the vast stores of theological erudition with which the pages of this ponderous work are filled.

More recent critics surmise that while the Abbé Coeur undoubtedly contributed much of raw material, the princess coordinated and edited the heterogeneous mass, imprinting her intellectual individuality upon the philosophical deductions, and suffusing its pages with the eclecticism of her personal convictions and faith. Monselet exclaims:

Les ouvrages de Madame la princesse de Belgiojoso, sont plutôt ceux d'un bénédictin que d'une femme du monde.

(The works of the Princess de Belgiojoso are rather those of a Benedictine than of a woman of the world.)

Lerminier, on the contrary, in a minute criticism, entitled *Des femmes philosophiques*, published the following June in the *Revue des Deux Mondes*, (1843), lashes unmercifully this attempt on the part of a woman of the world to penetrate the sacred realms of Philosophy, he carpingly exclaims:

What was our surprise, on finding that the *Essay on the Formation of the Christian Dogma*, is composed of a series of biographies, of extracts taken from the works of the Fathers of the Church, of narratives and quotations borrowed from the historians of the early Christian period ... together with an occasional analysis of the civil laws of the Longobards and the Teutons! Thus, instead of a book on the thought which underlies the Christian religion, we only have a *résumé* of external events. Metaphysics and theology should have provided the basis of the work, and it is biography which predominates. Between what the book promises and what it fulfils the contrast is such that it could not fail to escape the notice of the author herself. 'We greatly fear,' says Madame de Belgiojoso on reaching the end of her historical *résumé*, 'we greatly fear that we have not set forth in a satisfactory manner the first progressive steps of Catholic thought, that we have awkwardly confused men and things, and sometimes permitted the one to monopolise the attention we should have desired to bestow on the other.'

As this criticism which Madame de Belgiojoso herself so courageously directs to her work would seem to warrant, we will say without further evasion that the aim of her book is missed. Not an issue has been squarely faced and forced to a conclusion. The Christian dogma is not penetrated to its essence, nor is its course followed through the centuries. . . . The author of the *Essay on the Christian Dogma* declares that her opinions, confined within the limits fixed by the Church, are not intended for a moment to subsist in the face of any decrees the Church might see fit to issue hereafter.

We scarcely anticipate that a council will be convoked to sit in judgment on the doctrines of Madame de Belgiojoso; yet we doubt whether fervent Catholics will find in her book subject for edification. While professing an official submission to the decisions of the Church, Madame de Belgiojoso often gives evidence of a marked tendency towards scepticism. . . . The author has been accompanied in her researches by a deductive laxity which inclines her to assume a restive attitude towards orthodoxy, yet fails to inspire her with the courage necessary to philosophical independence.

Thus it is that one finds in the *Essay on the Formation of the Christian Dogma* neither the ardour of faith nor the daring of intellect: believers may be scandalised, but philosophers will not be satisfied. Nevertheless, the book has its merits. It is extraordinary that a woman should have taken the trouble to read or to skim so many historical documents, to analyse them, or have extracts made under her supervision. The style of the biographies, and of the notices of which the Essay is composed, is correct, elegant, and at times of a precision which tends to raise it to the gravity of history. Especially in the narration of political facts and theories does the author walk more firmly; yet even on that ground we could point out some strange errors.

The learned critic takes violent exception to the princess's estimate of the character of Saint Augustin, which he rightly considers treated with unwarrantable superficiality and prejudice, M. Lerminier protests:

Nous ignorons, si Madame de Belgiojoso avait résolu d'avance de trouver une victime parmi les pères de l'église; mais le choix a été malheureux.—*Revue des Deux Mondes,* January, 1843.
(We do not know whether Madame de Belgiojoso had resolved in advance to find a victim among the fathers of the church; But the choice was unfortunate.)

Sainte-Beuve, author of the famous *Lundis,* criticised the book in a letter to his friend, Madame Juste Olivier, at Lausanne:

It is thoughtful, catholic on the face; very strong and very simple in style; in fact, a very precious curiosity, coming as it does from the pen of a noble Italian, of a Trivulzio. Her name does not appear; but she acknowledges it. The work, so far, embraces the period extending from Saint Justin to Saint Augustin: two volumes are as yet unpublished.—*Correspondance de Sainte-Beuve avec M. et Mme. Juste Olivier.* Year 1843,

Despite the hostile criticism called forth by the *Essay on the Christian Dogma,* the publication of her later works guaranteed the Princess Belgiojoso a permanent place in the intellectual phalanx of her generation. Of these, the *Essai sur Vico* is perhaps the most characteristic. Her translation into French of the Neapolitan jurist, philosopher and critic's politico-historical work, *La Scienza Nuova,* dealing with a system of social (as distinguished from natural) theology—a demonstration of God's government of the world, and of the laws by which that government exists—bristling with obsolete and abstruse terminology and subtle technicalities, constitutes a *tour de force* which few experts could hope to surpass.

These volumes, the latter of which was issued in Paris in 1844, not only arrested the attention of specialists, but prepared the literary critics for the excellence of the political prose with which the same brilliant pen sought to galvanise popular interest, awake sympathy with the tribulations of her down-trodden compatriots, and perhaps secure a helping hand in their struggle for national regeneration.

An article entitled *Les Académies de Femmes en France*, published in the *Revue des Revues*, (December 15, 1899); and signed "*Une vieille Saint-Simonienne*," gives a curious account of the project formed by a group of Parisian bluestockings of founding an institute modelled after the famous French Academy, but composed exclusively of women. If we are to believe the writer, the Princess Belgiojoso was practically elected president of these Immortals. The struggle between the partisans of George Sand and Madame de Girardin, both ambitious of the coveted distinction, had been a fierce one, but ended in a deadlock. A compromise between the rival factions resulted in the selection of Princess Belgiojoso, in spite of her foreign birth. The writer of the article says:

> She was a woman of great patrician distinction, a passionate friend of G. Sand; a fierce zealot of the Republican Cause, her purse was liberally open to all political conspirators who had taken refuge in France, both Italian and French. Madame de Belgiojoso would certainly have made an exceptional president for the Woman's Academy: she was beautiful; of a tragic, impressive type; and her intelligence was great. Musset, in despair over the loss of G. Sand, made love to the princess in the hope of arousing Madame Sand's jealousy, and inducing her to return to him. . . . But George Sand and the princess laughed together over the naive Machiavellian intrigues of the amorous swain, and encouraged his illusions; for Madame Sand was not ill-pleased to follow all the phases of this curious experimental romance, and thus continue the study, through the intercession of her friend, of the complex nature of their genial victim, who became a puppet, a subject for dissection, in the hands of two women, both psychologists of the first order.

Madame de Girardin soon appreciated the fact that in face of the support given Madame de Belgiojoso the defeat of her own ambitions was certain. Furious over her discomfiture, she wrote those corrosive chronicles which go to make up the twaddle of her book, *Le Vicomte de Launay*. The grapes were sour, so she spurned them, taking her revenge by means of the ridicule she heaped on the whole scheme of the proposed Academy—forgetting, or disdainfully ignoring, the fact that she herself had been one of the most energetic instigators of the plan while her own chances of securing the presidency had been in the ascendant. In her desire for vengeance Madame de Girardin did not stop short at ridiculing the Academy. The author of the article cited continues:

Fearful of her personal chagrin becoming too noticeable, she caused Madame de Belgiojoso to be attacked with the most incredible virulence by several of her allies in the world of letters. Thus, in the *Croix de Berny* (letter iii.), she traitorously inserted, in a passage signed Théophile Gautier, an atrocious portrait of the Italian princess; a portrait which assured for this otherwise tiresome volume a huge *succès de scandale* throughout Parisian society.

The princess's friends and adherents remained faithful in spite of the tempest raised by her adversaries. In vain Donna Christina, dismayed by the insults heaped upon her, declined to push her claims. Madame Ancelot, determined that their mutual foes should be made to bite the dust, worked for the reluctant candidate with might and main. Some preliminary meetings actually took place: not in the sumptuous halls of the Palais Castellane, as had been at first proposed, but in the more humble and austere Athenaeum of the Rue de Valois. The change was made (probably at the suggestion of the princess) in order to more fully accentuate the frankly democratic significance it was the desire of members to impart to the labours of the assembly.

Interest soon flagged, however, when the glamour of strife had departed; and the much-heralded *Académie des Femmes* died an inglorious death.

Another distinguished Italian exile, Count Cesare Balbo, had just published (1844) a book destined to exert an immense influence, and which appealed strongly to the princess. In his *Le Speranze d'Italia* Balbo presented the Italian problem with statesmanlike foresight and moderation. Discarding the spasmodic and futile efforts of disconnected conspiracy, he advocated the gradual political education of the people. Before an efficient blow could be struck for national independence, Italian rulers and their subjects must, he urged, become imbued with a spirit of mutual confidence and a real appreciation of the solidarity of their mutual interests. The arguments were especially pointed at the Kingdom of Sardinia, and the possibilities which the general condition of Italian politics offered the Savoy dynasty; but they could be made to fit the requirements and ambitions of other Italian States.

Princess Belgiojoso, who had founded and practically supported a periodical designed for the propaganda of just such theories, enthusiastically welcomed the new apostle. Although she maintained her personal friendship with Mazzini, fully alive to the nobility of his character and the purity of his motives, the princess no longer shared the convictions which formed the pivot on which the political schemes of the Genoese agitator revolved.

The futility of the mouthings of a handful of conspirators and political malcontents banded together in secret conclave, but lacking popular support, had long since become apparent. The lesson taught by Mazzini's rash and blundering expedition of 1833 had very effectually opened her eyes as to the value of either the political information or penetration possessed by the over-sanguine insurrectionist. Yet she reverenced the splendid abnegation of the individual and the patriot, while she deplored the stubborn intractability of the politician, and to the end denied him neither her affectionate esteem nor the homage to which his personal sufferings, endured in a noble cause, so amply entitled him.

Prince Belgiojoso had followed his wife to Paris, and, when the release of their Italian property permitted a mode of life in accordance with their exalted social station, he established himself in an apartment under the same roof. How far La Fayette had been instrumental in effecting a reconciliation is unknown, but we are aware how anxious he was that the young couple should arrange their differences. On December 23, 1838, a daughter was born to the princess. The responsibilities of motherhood would seem to have weighed lightly with Donna Christina at this period, although ten or twelve years later the maternal instinct awakened to moments of fitful activity.

The tall and graceful figure of the prince was frequently seen at the brilliant gatherings in his wife's *salons*. As has been said, Don Emilio possessed a voice which was the admiration and delight of the musical world of his day. Privileged contemporaries have left records of the enthusiasm created when the prince, with Bellini or Rossini at the piano, held his audience spellbound, transporting his enraptured hearers to realms where melody reigned supreme.

Poor young Bellini! The gifted composer of *Norma*, *Puritani*, *Sonambula*, and other operas which still hold the stage today, was not always at his ease in the house of his friend and protector. Another distinguished guest, the cynical and brilliant Heinrich Heine, invariably singled out the timid youth as his especial butt, turning into ridicule, despite the amiable intervention of the hostess, the *gaucheries* of the Sicilian genius. Like many of his compatriots, Vincenzo Bellini was morbidly superstitious.

Aware of this infirmity, for it really amounted to such, the malignant Heine one day prostrated his timorous victim with the prophecy—supported by such examples as Mozart, Pergolese, Raphael, and others—that genius died young, and that as such Bellini must be prepared to quit the scene of his triumphs at an early date. Shaking in every limb, the terrified Bellini, exorcising the Evil Eye with extended index and little finger, incontinently fled. Within a week (September 24, 1835) the unfortunate youth, deeply mourned by the prince and princess, and by the inconsolable Rossini, who loved him as a son, succumbed to a sudden intestinal disorder.

The intimacy of Belgiojoso with Rossini was of many years standing. In Milan, during the early youth of the dashing aristocrat, the composer had been amongst his closest friends, and a fervent admirer of his magnificent voice. Madame Jaubert relates, (*Souvenirs de Madame Jaubert*), a discussion which took place in her presence between Berryer, the great French advocate and politician, and the prince concerning the rival merits of Meyerbeer and Rossini. Belgiojoso maintained that their very methods of composition sufficed to determine their relative artistic value, for whereas the one took years in the development and construction of his work, with the other inspiration and execution were practically simultaneous. The prince cried:

> The opera *Tancrede*, was written in six days at my Villa Pliniana on Lake Como, during the course of a shooting party. When we returned to the villa, worn out by a ten-hour tramp in the woods, Rossini, sitting at the corner of the table awaiting supper, used to scribble his little notes on loose sheets of paper. Then, at dessert, seating himself at a small piano placed close at hand, he would call out, 'Come, Emilio, and you, Pompeo'— my cousin, who had a magnificent bass voice—'come, my children, let us try this!' And then we would set about deciphering the cramped hieroglyphics, the Master himself supplying all the missing parts.
>
> We attacked the chorus with all the power of our lungs, fancying that we thus obtained an idea of the full effect. Then Rossini would return to his corner of the table to scribble corrections or add more sheets. The interest we took in it all kept us awake.

VINCENZO BELLINI

Besides, we almost believed that we were ourselves composing the music. At last we went to bed; but Pompeo always had us up by six, and we began shooting again without further thought of *Tancrede* until evening. The original manuscript score of that opera I have carefully preserved in the Palazzo Belgiojoso in Milan.

Music and political intrigue this ill-assorted couple enjoyed in common, but these constituted the only bonds which held them together. At their home, all the great musicians of the day found an enthusiastic welcome and an appreciative audience. Here Chopin, Thalberg, Liszt, Rossini, and Bellini, together with Grisi, Mario—greatest of tenors—and a host of lesser lights, lavished their respective talents with a reckless prodigality engendered by the intoxicating artistic ambient.

Even during the most fervent period of her religious exaltation and mysticism, while she was compiling those imposing volumes on the Catholic Dogma, the princess did not forego the languorous raptures afforded her by the voices of the great singers at the Italian Opera. Her lithe form, slim almost to emaciation, draped in the ashen-hued tunic of the Grey Sisters, a religious order founded in Paris in 1617, her dark tresses circled with a garland of pond-lilies, she must indeed have presented a fantastic figure as she reclined rather than sat in her opera box. Overcome by the emotional tension which reacted on her delicate nerves, Donna Christina had frequently to be carried in the arms of a friend from the theatre to her conveyance.

The friendship with Heine dated from the early years of her sojourn in Paris, when she was frequently seen in General La Fayette's *salons*. Here, probably in 1831, the author of the *Buch der Lieder* and the *Reisebilder* first experienced the peculiar fascination this remarkable woman exerted over all—or nearly all, for there were some notable exceptions—who approached her. Among these exceptions was Balzac, who remained obdurately recalcitrant. Writing to Madame Hanska, the creator of *La Comédie Humaine* frankly expresses his dislike of the princess:

> "*Elle a le bonheur de me déplaire . . . Sa maison est bien tenue; on y fait de l'esprit. J'y suis allé deux samedis; j'y ai dîné une fois; ce sera tout.*"—G. Ferry, *Balzac et ses amis.*
> (She has the good fortune to displease me. . . His house is well kept; There is spirit in it. I went there two Saturdays; I dined

PRINCESS BELGIOJOSO

there once; that's it.)

The famous painter Delacroix shared Balzac's opinion. Alfred de Musset, at one time her slave, became her most insidious detractor. Wounded vanity was, however, the incentive of his lyrical revenge. But of this later. Heine showed a different spirit. Madly in love with the beautiful Italian, who received his amorous homage with scornful indifference, yet encouraged and cultivated his friendship, the German accepted defeat and forgot his resentment in his enjoyment of the intellectual privileges afforded by the society of his Egeria.

In the estimation of a recent French critic, M. Jules Legras, (*Henri Heine,* Paris, 1897), the two women who exercised the most potent influences over Heinrich Heine, in so far as the shaping of his destinies was concerned, were the Princess Belgiojoso, his protectress, and Mathilde Mirat, his mistress and eventually his wife.

Politics first awakened a fellow-feeling. Like the princess, Heine was an exile who had come to Paris in order to wage untrammelled the struggle for the political emancipation of his own country. The fidelity of the poet-politician to the principles he professed was, however, now and again in danger of collapse, for his was not the uncompromising hostility which welcomes martyrdom as the consummation of sacrifice to a political ideal. From Aix, he writes to his enchantress (October 30, 1836):

> Shall I, *Madame,* soon make my peace—an ignoble peace— with the authorities beyond the Rhine, in order to be free of the worries of exile and from these tedious straits which are worse than absolute poverty? Alas! the temptations are becoming great of late. . . . I have more frankness than those who like to style themselves a Brutus or a Regulus; have I not?

Yet a moment later he catches himself up, fearful lest he forfeit the friendship of his princess by this lamentable display of poltroonery, ascribing his hesitations to a "malady of the soul" rather than to physical irresolution.

The letter closes with this glowing tribute, fulsome in its vapid adulation:

> Yours is the most complete personality I have found on earth. Yes! Before I knew you, I imagined that persons like you, endowed with all the perfections of body and mind, existed only in fairy tales, or in the dreams of poets. Now I know that the

Ideal is not a mere chimera: that a Reality corresponds to our most sublime Imaginings; and when thinking of you, princess, I sometimes cease to doubt another Divinity which I was also prone to relegate to the realm of my dreams.—Legras, *op. cit.*

To Heine, still hampered by the Teutonism his secret soul would fain discard, the associations formed in the brilliant atmosphere of the Belgiojoso's *salon* were of inestimable value. The princess had succeeded in surrounding herself with a marvellously select circle of politicians, writers, savants, artists, and musicians; men and women conspicuous for learning, wit, and beauty. Comparisons have been made between her salon and that of Madame Récamier, both brilliant examples of the social-intellectual life of the period, although the latter lived on rather by virtue of the hostess's connection with an historic epoch. (E. Herriot, *Madame Récamier et ses amis*; M. Muret in *Revue Bleue,* July 12, 1902.)

At one time or another the *habitués* of the princess's famous Saturdays included the ever-devoted Thiers; the historians Mignet and Augustin Thierry; Alfred de Musset and his brother Paul; Victor Cousin, the philosopher; George Sand; "Stendhal" (Henry Beyle); Victor Hugo; the "Most Gorgeous" Lady Blessington; the Countess Guiccioli (of Byronic fame); Mrs. Trollope; de Tocqueville (whose *Democratic en Amérique* had obtained immediate success); Alexandre Dumas, the elder; Théophile Gautier, and scores of less well-known names. Mention has been made of the musical element which distinguished these gatherings; but there was a period when philosophy held an equally prominent place, and again an epoch when politics absorbed them both.

Whatever Paris contained of note—native or foreign—eagerly sought an introduction. Rarely has a foreigner created such a sensation in French society, or excited polite curiosity to a like degree. The princess incarnated paradox. She was never *banale*: nor was she ever vulgar. Far-fetched as her eccentricities of *toilette* and surroundings undoubtedly were; childish as seemed her continual pose and reaching after effect, no action of hers was wholly bereft of distinction, even of dignity. Her intellectual culture and patriotic fire; her artistic extravagance; her fierce and tireless energy and picturesque languor; all contributed to the exceptional position she held.

Elle fut avec plus de flamme ce que Madame du Deffand avait été*, au XVIIIe siècle, avec plus d'esprit; et vingt ans plus tôt, Madame*

Récamier, avec plus de majesté: elle fut un centre. . . . Personne ne fit plus qu'elle, en France, pour la propagation de l'idée italienne. Elle lui consacra sa vie, sa fortune, son coeur."

(It was with more flame what Madame de Deffand had been more witty in the eighteenth century; And twenty years before, Madame Recamier, with more majesty: she was a center. . . . No one did more than she did in France for the propagation of the Italian idea. She devoted her life, her fortune, her heart.)

Thus, Hanotaux describes the Princess Belgiojoso in his critical biography of the French historian Henri Martin, whose sympathetic interest in the aspirations of her beloved Italy endeared him to the exile.

A portrait penned by that inveterate *boulevardier*, Arsène Houssaye, is interesting as showing the sphinx in the glare of realism under which the "man in the street" is wont to dissect his "type." Houssaye's sketch, shorn of symbolism, and impregnated with subtle irony, depicts the princess as he knew her, or heard her discussed. His language is that affected by the literary Bohemia to which he belonged; it is that of the Quartier Latin and the Boulevards, and as such incomprehensible to most who dwell beyond those classic precincts. We have therefore rendered it into English, preserving the spirit when the wording defied literal translation:—

Among faces which have left on me the strongest impression, is that of the Princess Belgiojoso. None could fail to be struck by the Byzantine pallor of her skin; by her hair, black as the raven's wing; by her beautiful luminous eyes—great windows in the facade of a little palace. Some objected (playing upon the significance of her name), '*belle et joyeuse, parcequ'elle n'est ni belle ni joyeuse.*' No, not joyful; but beautiful assuredly to those who looked upon her through the eyes of Art. Madame de Girardin was the tenth Muse, but the Princess Belgiojoso was the Romantic Muse.

As is known, at that time every romantic woman boasted a spectral pallor; a rosy complexion was unfashionable, and as such left to the old school, with the sneer that the owner could never have known what passion meant; but all those who were haunted by visions of Shakespeare, Hugo, or Dumas, never ventured into society unadorned by some bluish-greenish blend of hue. It was said that the Princess Belgiojoso stimulated her brain through the medium of a fashionable poison, *datura stramonium.* They did not use rat poison in those days. The princess was an enthusiastic votary of habits nocturnal, and astonished Paris by the originality of her ways.

Every woman is more or less like an oft-read book. This one was, however, a quite new volume: one took it up, but little by little, after the first pages written in French or in Italian, one stumbled on Hebrew. Did she understand herself when she posed alternately as a type of the Italian Renaissance, as a romantic *Signora*, as the Muse of Romanticism? A perverted mind housed in an impeccable body! Alfred de Musset wasted his second youth in her toils.

At first she took one's breath away, but soon she charmed one. She possessed that penetrating femininity peculiar to the Milanese; yet unfortunately the apostle too often overshadowed the woman, for she wanted to reform the world! Tall, graceful, her face was ideally modelled: the nose arched, slightly aquiline; the nostrils mobile and passionate, the mouth full, with lips which held great promise. Beautiful when smiling, the mouth appeared set when grave.

Why did the princess prefer to show a brow clouded with thought rather than lips full of sentiment? Alas! it was her destiny. The prince preferred amiable women; the princess made pretence to the character of a man. Fortunately, she had her moments of natural relaxation. Although her pride was glacial, her curiosity was keen, and she bravely risked an occasional stumble in Parisian pitfalls. Alfred de Musset accused her of loving herself only, but some women suspected her of hiding her game.—*Confessions*, vol. ii.

There is more in the same vein, but for the nonce this sample will serve our purpose.

Among her friends the princess counted Guizot, Michelet, and Thierry—a trio of France's most revered historians. For Augustin Thierry, even then stricken with blindness, she entertained a cult composed in equal parts of admiration and compassionate affection. Charles Monselet writes:

The profound friendship which united the Princess Belgiojoso with the author of *The Conquest of England* is one of the most beautiful and noble spectacles we have beheld.

This alliance between active thought and inward reflection, between the knight and the hermit, between action and repose, is every day fruitful in potent results. The one goes forth and makes history, the other remains to chronicle.—*Statues et Statuettes.*

A pavilion in the garden of the princess's home in the Rue de Montparnasse was reserved for the exclusive use of the blind historian. Here he, whom Chateaubriand called the "Homer of History," spent his declining years, cheered and encouraged by his benefactress's intellectual sympathy no less than by the gracious solicitude which watched over his physical infirmity.

Monsieur Casimir Stryienski has in his collection a charming note in the hand of the princess, addressed to Jean A. Letronne, the Egyptologist, thanking the author for a memoir on Egyptian civilisation which he had recently sent her. After expressing astonishment at the ease with which the learned explorer penetrates the dark places of a lost civilisation, guiding his readers with consummate skill, she exclaims:

Merci donc, Monsieur, de m'avoir procuré un plaisir assez rare aujourd'hui: celui d'admirer avec sécurité.
(Thank you, Sir, for having given me a rare pleasure today: that of admiring with security.)

Could a more subtle compliment be conveyed? But we have quoted the letter on account of its reference to Thierry, the note continues:

I would be charmed, should the remembrance you have kept of me be sufficiently keen to induce you to climb the Rue de Courcelles. My friend Thierry would rejoice equally with me. If you could spare us an evening, you would find us together surrounded by a few friends; for it is in the evening that he permits himself conversation, and he enjoys it as being the only distraction left to him.—Dated May 23, 1845.

The Princess Belgiojoso had been received by Madame Récamier shortly after her arrival in Paris, and the acquaintance ripened into such intimacy as the great discrepancy in their ages allowed. A delicate charm still clung to the personality of the famous beauty of the Consulate and Empire. Unlike many a society queen, Madame Récamier disdained all subterfuge, accepting with a dignified resignation the ravages of time. The *salon* of the Abbaye-aux-Bois was between

1830-1845 a living force in literary circles, the hall-mark of its approval carrying quite as much weight as the applause of the *coterie* of the University or of the *Revue des Deux Mondes*.

It was nicknamed the antechamber of the French Academy: certainly, more than one of the "Immortals" owed his elevation to that august assemblage to the influences exerted by the Fairy Godmother who, decked out in gossamer white and soft-hued muslins, presided over the discussions of her brilliant guests. With the Belgiojoso she loved to evoke the recollections of her Italian triumphs: how she had posed for Canova in Rome; and the childlike effusions with which the people of the Eternal City—still Pagan in its worship of the beautiful in Art or Nature—greeted her every appearance in public.

Surrounded by old friends such as Châteaubriand and Balanche, and by the younger generation represented by Mérimée, Alfred de Vigny, Sainte-Beuve, &c., the evening of her eventful life was spent with exquisite serenity, until abruptly closed during the terrible cholera scourge of 1849, when the fell disease claimed her among its victims.

The intimacy of the Princess Belgiojoso with George Sand, her senior by but four years, was, on the other hand, cemented not only by a community of tastes in literature and art, but by deep sympathy with the burning social and political problems of the day. The two women were indeed well fitted to understand and appreciate each other. The author of *Indiana* made no secret of her admiration for the Italian exile, whose political creed and noble aspirations for the regeneration of the proletariat she shared, while in the Milanese patrician she found a kindred spirit in her attitude of contempt for the social conventionalities.

A fervent disciple of Mazzini, George Sand (Madame Dudevant) was instrumental in the furtherance of his propaganda, and the spread in France of his social theories. Temperamentally as far removed as the magnetic poles, the two friends never clashed in spite of the intrigues of a mutual admirer; for although the Frenchwoman might marvel, she could but admire the marble-like frigidity which repulsed the amorous ardour of an Alfred de Musset.

For the genius of de Musset the princess professed unbounded enthusiasm. Unfortunately, their friendship was not of long duration. Unfortunately, because having been successful at one period in aiding him during a fit of discouragement and despondency, her influence, if continued, might have maintained the poet on the heights to which his genius occasionally soared, only to be dragged to earth

71

again through the frailty of his moral nature. To such a man friendship with so beautiful a woman was impossible: it must be either love or hate, and the disdain of his fair enchantress quickly turned his tender sentiment to one of deep resentment. The princess wrote de Musset,

> The penalty of vulgar amours, is the denial to those who indulge in them of aspirations towards a noble love.

And in the same breath she significantly alludes to *des succès faciles*; an insinuation which enraged the sensitive poet, and deeply wounded a fastidious vanity fed on the adulation of Parisian drawing-rooms. De Musset is cited as acknowledging:

> I was for a week between her velvet paws, and I still preserve the traces in my imagination, I won't say my heart, for the claws never penetrated so deep. . . .—De Janzé *Alfred de Musset.*

Quarrels between the princess and her poet were of frequent occurrence; we are, however, inclined to attach but a minor importance to the incident provoked by de Musset's caricatures, which are by some believed to have occasioned the final breach. It would be to misunderstand our heroine's character, proud and vain though she undoubtedly was, to believe that she would have sacrificed a friend whose genius she admired and whose attentions flattered her sense of personal importance, for no other reason than this childish impertinence of his.

The caricatures have been reproduced in the volume of anecdotes on de Musset and his friends, published by the Vicomtesse de Janzé. (*Récits sur de Musset.*) They are very rough sketches; the drawing is childish, grotesque even; but it would be far-fetched indeed to style them insulting, in spite of the "horrible resemblance" detected by some. Nor can we discover anything wilfully insulting in the lines in de Musset's hand, traced beneath them:

> *Pallida, sed quamvis pallida, pulchra tamen.*
> (Pale but although pale, yet beautiful.)

What woman, having pretensions for wit and intellect, would proclaim herself outraged by such a trivial lapse of good taste! No, the reasons which prompted the final and definite estrangement between the poet and his idol must be sought elsewhere.

Paul de Musset, in his interesting biography of his famous brother, relates that during an illness which laid the poet low the Princess Belgiojoso, "who never lost an opportunity of doing good," came several times to visit the sufferer. With her own hand she administered the potions, which the invalid "dared not refuse to take when offered by so great a lady." The biographer continues:

One day, when he was feeling particularly ill, the princess re-marked with the utmost assurance, 'Calm yourself; no one ever dies in my presence.'

From a feeling of gratitude he made as if he believed her, but when she promised to return on the morrow it was in perfect sincerity that he whispered, "Then I shall not die on that day." (*Biographie d'Alfred de Musset, par Paul de Musset.*)

Paul de Musset places this episode towards the close of the year 1841; and he deplores the departure of his brother's friend, he continues:

The Princess Belgiojoso, whose *salon* was one of the most agreeable of Paris, was to spend the winter in Italy. There she made a noble use of her great fortune, founding, a few leagues from Milan, a large charitable institution. Like Soeur Marcel-line (his brother's nurse), she had talked very seriously to the poet. Alfred wrote to this beautiful counsellor to tell her how much he missed the affectionate chidings to which her words lent such sweetness that, in order to hear them again, he would willingly suffer another illness. The princess replied inviting him to seek in Italy a softer climate, a healthful diet, together with other subjects of poetical inspiration than those offered by the Boulevard de Gand. She promised him complete liberty, a spacious apartment, a family library full of rare books, and as many scoldings as he might desire. This gracious invitation filled him with joy and gratitude. Often during the winter of 1841, he repeated, 'I am not forgotten by everybody. When I bore myself too much here, I know where to find a welcome.' But although in Paris he talked of going to Italy, he wrote to Milan that the proposed journey was a dream.—*Op. cit.*

Amongst the various documents which we have been privileged to examine, there is no record of a journey to Italy during the winter of 1841-42. Nevertheless, as the princess was a beneficiary under the provisions of the amnesty granted political offenders by the Emperor Ferdinand on his accession in 1838, nothing would have prevented a

ALFRED DE MUSSET.

visit to her native city; indeed, her husband did take advantage of the Imperial clemency.

Be this as it may, the year 1842 was to witness the end of the romantic intimacy existing between the princess and the too susceptible poet. His brother writes:

"He was then deeply interested in a very beautiful and very great lady, for whom he entertained a great affection, but who treated him at times with a harshness and a severity he did not always patiently endure; as a consequence, this friendship was frequently disturbed by storms and quarrels. I never knew what the subject of complaint was; but he must have suffered some particularly harsh, wounding, and unjust treatment on the day he came home, determined to end it once and for all. It was while in this frame of mind that he wrote the verses *Sur une Morte*. The rupture was absolute, irremediable. In order to determine whether the author of these verses committed a fault, it would be necessary to have full knowledge of the nature of the affront, of the wound he had received, and nobody knows how serious it may have been. No one blamed the great Corneille because he yielded to an impulse of poetic anger against a woman who had been guilty of the imprudence of mocking him. The way to avoid the lion's claws is not to irritate him."—Paul de Musset, *op. cit.*

The offending verses with which the poet turned upon his arrogant tormentor, stigmatising her heartlessness, appeared in the *Revue des Deux Mondes* on June 1, 1842. (The poem is erroneously dated *October* in Lemerre's edition of de Mussel's works.)

SUR UNE MORTE
Elle était belle, si la Nuit
Qui dort dans la sombre chapelle
Où Michel-Ange a fait son lit,
Immobile peut être belle.
(She was beautiful, if the Night
Who sleeps in the sombre chapel
Where Michelangelo made her bed,
Motionless, can be beautiful.)

Elle était bonne, s'il suffit
Qu'en passant la main s'ouvre et donne,
Sans que Dieu n'ait rien vu, rien dit,
Si l'or sans pitié fait l'aumône.
(She was good, if it's enough

That in passing the hand opens and gives,
Without God having seen anything, said anything,
If gold without pity makes alms.)

Elle pensait, si le vain bruit
D'une voix douce et cadencée,
Comme le ruisseau qui gémit
Peut faire croire à la pensée.
(She thought, if the idle noise
Of a sweet and cadenced voice
Like the brook that burbles
Can make you believe in thought.)

Elle priait, si deux beaux yeux,
Tantôt s'attachant à la terre,
Tantôt se levant vers les cieux,
Peuvent s'appeler la Prière.
(She prayed, if two beautiful eyes,
Now fixing on the ground,
Now lifting towards the heavens,
Can be called Prayer.)

Elle aurait souri, si la fleur
Qui ne s'est point épanoui
Pouvait s'ouvrir à la fraicheur
Du vent qui passe et qui l'oublie.
(She would have smiled, if the flower
That hasn't bloomed at all
Could open itself to the freshness
Of the wind that passes and forgets it.)

Elle aurait pleuré si sa main,
Sur son cœur froidement posée,
Eût jamais, dans l'argile humain,
Senti la céleste rosée.
(She would have wept if her hand,
Placed coldly on her heart,
Had ever, in human clay,
Felt the heavenly dew.)

Elle aurait aimé, si l'orgueil
Pareil à la lampe inutile
Qu'on allume près d'un cercueil,
N'eût veillé sur son cœur stérile.

(She would have loved, if pride
Like the useless lamp
That we light near a coffin,
Had not kept vigil over her sterile heart.)

Elle est morte, et n'a point vécu.
Elle faisait semblant de vivre.
De ses mains est tombé le livre
Dans lequel elle n'a rien lu.
(She is dead, and hasn't lived at all.
She made an appearance of living.
From her hands is fallen the book
In which she has read nothing.)

The publication of these verses made a great stir. All Paris had gossiped over the infatuation of the poet for the beautiful foreigner. Ill-natured comment was rife concerning this sudden and inexplicable change of front. But the lyrical vengeance of her former adorer appeared to leave the princess quite indifferent. If she was wounded, her haughty character forbade any sign which might betray her annoyance. She is reported to have nonchalantly questioned a casual visitor as to whether she had read the verses about which everyone was talking.

"It seems that the prototype is Rachel," remarked the princess.

"Yes, it must be Mademoiselle Rachel," assented her interlocutor, with a malicious smile, and glancing archly at the impassive Italian, "because I heard Mademoiselle Rachel say to Buloz (editor of the *Revue des Deux Mondes*), 'So you have published those verses which Alfred de Musset dedicated to the Princess Belgiojoso!'"

Madame Adam, commenting on this incident observes:

Men revenge themselves cruelly on women who have shown more passion in their devotion to ideas than to love: for it constitutes a species of theft to their detriment.

And she goes on to relate that the Princess Belgiojoso, to whom she was introduced by a mutual friend, has ever remained one of her greatest admirations, she adds:

She loved Italy ardently, faithfully, till her death, she lived exclusively for her country, and consecrated her beauty, her intellect, and her fortune to that one end. . . . The Princess Belgiojoso is one of the noblest types of womanhood Europe produced in the last century. From 1848 to 1860 she was an incomparable heroine.—*Mes premières armes littéraires et politiques.*

We find no further record of any intercourse between the princess and de Musset for several years. Then, suddenly, after seeing his play, *Louison*, she writes, addressing her note to the care of the poet's brother, Paul:

I cannot resist telling you that you have created *un petit chef-d'oeuvre.* Your *Louison* is admirable, full of grace and of sincerity, of delicacy and sentiment. You think and feel like Shakespeare, and you express yourself like Marivaux; it is a strange amalgamation, of which the effect is striking. Perhaps you no longer remember my existence; never mind, you have found a certain way of perpetuating your own memory, even in the mind of the most forgetful of beings. I thank you for the delightful moments I owe you.

Christine Trivulce De Belgiojoso.
(February, 1849, quoted by Mme. Martellet in her *Alfred de Musset intime.*)

For many years a close companionship existed between de Musset and Prince Emilio Belgiojoso. By some it is averred that the consequences of this friendship were detrimental to the complete development of the poet's unquestionable genius, and that for the direct causes of his physical degeneration resulting in his premature death the Italian nobleman bears a heavy moral responsibility. Possessed of Herculean strength, the fast and reckless life seemed to have no hold upon Don Emilio's magnificent physique; but with de Musset it was otherwise. Cavour, who paid his first visit to Paris in 1837, and who was speedily initiated into the life led by the prince and his set, records several of their orgies.

After a lively dinner at the Café de Paris, the future statesman and maker of Italy, entering an account of the evening in the pages of his diary, exclaims in mock despair:

Me voila donc enrôlé parmi les plus mauvais sujets de Paris!
(So here I am enlisted among the worst subjects of Paris!)

But there was a deeper side to the question which did not escape the keen intelligence of the great Italian.

All those (exiles) I knew personally saddened me to the depths of my heart, offering the spectacle of great capacities doomed to sterility and impotency.—Chiala, *Lettere di Cavour, i.*

Doomed, moreover, by no fault of their own, but crushed under the weight of a jealous Absolutism which dreaded the ascendency of any intellect seeking to raise the dignity of the citizen above the dead-level of ignorance by virtue of which alone it battened. Cavour does not appear to have been attracted by the princess at this period, although he occasionally frequented her house.

The Princess Belgiojoso had talent and learning, she knew nearly all the men of any name in literature, art, and politics, but in her conversation she was now hostile to the House of Savoy, now favourable to it; at one moment superlatively antagonistic to, at another the advocate of, the most fantastic schemes.

As a consequence, we read, under date of January 27 (1838), the following words in the hand of Count Cavour:

On ne m'y reprendra plus. (I will not be taken back.)—D. Berti, *Il Conte de Cavour avanti il* 1848.

Generous to a fault, Prince Belgiojoso rivalled even his wife in the tactful and liberal relief he extended in the financial embarrassments of his friends among Italian exiles. But, as might be inferred from his manner of life, active participation in the political schemes for his country's regeneration ceased when the fatal routine of pleasure and debauch held Don Emilio in its grasp. Contemporaries are unanimous in classing the prince among the most popular and influential worldlings of the Paris of his day. His really great musical gifts, which ranked him with the professional talent of Europe; the charm and intellectuality of his conversation; the grace and elegance of his person; perhaps his widespread reputation for naughtiness, endeared him to a very large and cosmopolitan circle.

Inconsistent, except in his pleasures, Don Emilio took advantage of the free pardon offered political offenders on the accession of the Emperor Ferdinand to attend the coronation ceremonies of 1838 in Milan. The *salon* of Prince Metternich, who had accompanied the Court, became the rendezvous of that faction of the Lombard aristocracy which was willing to forget 1821 and 1830 for the sake of basking in the Imperial favour. On one occasion, Rossini being at the piano, Belgiojoso held the brilliant assembly enthralled.

"What a voice!" cried the Princess Metternich in a transport of enthusiasm.

"And what a loss to music if your husband had had me executed," added Belgiojoso, with piquancy. (Hübner, *Une Année de ma vie*.)

Needless to say, that this sarcastic reference to the conspiracies in which he had delighted, and in which his wife was still so deeply involved, was received with embarrassed silence. It was a period of conciliation indeed, but not of reconciliation, although the blandishments of an Imperial Court might temporarily dazzle and lure a minority of the pleasure-loving aristocracy.

Although frequently to be met in his wife's salon, especially when great lights of the musical world were present, the prince and princess practically lived in different worlds. As has been said, art alone struck any chord of sympathy between them. This strange woman, haunted by dreams and spiritual voices like a modern Joan of Arc; whose sentiency and enthusiasms were reserved for abstract principles and political theories; possessed but scant attraction for the frank materialism of Emilio Belgiojoso. Yet the fault lay not entirely on his side. His subsequent life demonstrated convincingly that he was capable of a constancy, a singleness of devotion almost without parallel in romantic records of recent times.

The obscure processes of the intellectual and psychological growth of the fantastic self-willed being who, in her chrysalis state, he had made his wife, and who now in the full development of her extraordinary personality bade defiance to husband and world alike, were, to this self-indulgent, pleasure-loving rake not only incomprehensible but supremely irritating. Temperamentally antagonistic, a fundamental incompatibility engendered mutual intolerance.

The intermittent patriotism of the prince, indulged in as might be some hazardous sport the zest of which lay in the pleasurable excitement of danger, even his careless generosity to the exiles who crossed his path, counted for little in the eyes of the fanatic for freedom, whose veneration for the ethics and abstract principles of the creed she professed was uncompromisingly dogmatic. Jealousy had been one of the earlier factors in the ever-widening domestic breach. Don Emilio's careless neglect of his young wife during the first months of their married life had aroused her resentment, inflamed her pride, and intensified her inherent insensibility.

The passivity of her physical nature only became more accentuated with the expansion and development of her intellectual faculties; and although a real, if peculiar, friendship existed between husband and wife, it is doubtful whether the notorious misconduct of the prince after 1830, or even the final catastrophe, deeply influenced the princess, much as it outraged her pride. The sting in de Musset's cruel verses lay, perhaps, in the knowledge of her own limitations and a vague appreciation of the psychic incompleteness such restrictions implied. Infinitely compassionate towards the physical and moral sufferings of humanity and deeply interested in their alleviation, the Princess Belgiojoso from the frigid heights whither her indifference and deceptions led her, looked down half contemptuous, half yearning, upon the sentiment the poet glorified. Much coveted, much loved, Christina Belgiojoso reciprocated the passion of none, although in many instances she retained the friendship of her adorers.

The *Journal* of Doctor Prosper Méniére has recently been published by his son. (*Journal du Docteur Prosper Méniére.*) This physician filled during the middle of the last century a somewhat analogous social position to that held by Doctor Tronchin in Geneva in Voltaire's time; that is to say, he frequented the best society, and was thoroughly in touch with its political and literary elements.

The doctor, under date of February 9, 1855, writes:

The other evening, at Madame de Boigne's, we were sitting in the *salon*, when the talk turned on Madame la Princesse de Belgiojoso (à *propos* of a recent article of hers in the *Revue des Deux Mondes*, entitled "*La Vie nomade, les Turcs, &c.*") This lady became the subject of a lengthy conversation, and as it was one of interest, I may, perhaps, be permitted to give some details.

The chronicler then proceeds to relate many facts concerning the princess's career, which have already been set forth in these pages, and which, consequently, need not be repeated. Méniére assures his readers, on what authority we know not, that it was owing to her intimacy with Mignet, and to the very considerable influence he exerted with various members of the Diplomatic Corps, that the princess regained possession of her income, which, as has been stated, was confiscated by the Austrian Government.

This income Méniére places at £8,000 a year—a large one for that period, he continues:

She had a charming house in the Faubourg Saint-Honoré, and there she gave asylum to her husband, in a little apartment over the stables, *quoique les époux fussent séparés de corps et de biens*, (although the spouses were separated from bodies and property.)

Madame de Belgiojoso occupied herself with serious philosophical and religious studies. She published a treatise on the Fathers of the Church—a remarkable work, it is said. She was at that time very intimate with a theologian, and the gossips have it that the learned man lent a hand. Nevertheless, there are well-informed persons who maintain the contrary, and affirm that the lady needed the help of none in order to astonish the world with an achievement so foreign to the habits of the fair sex. This philosophical work brought her great honour.

But her favourites succeeded each other, and comment grew apace. Liszt, a madcap if ever there was one, became her constant companion; then came M. Libri; then this one, and then that. In short, there were enough to keep Parisian tongues wagging for many years. I remember having seen in the studio of a young painter, a pupil of M. Ingres, a magnificent portrait of the aforesaid princess. She was clothed entirely in white, like a Vestal, and her face, of a deadly pallor, conveyed very exactly the idea of a spectre.

It was very distinguished, but, according to my taste, very unpleasant. Never was fantasy allowed greater rein. It was a challenge thrown to all, and the artist, mad over his model, had lent the magic of his talent to the eccentricities of the sitter. All means were good to her provided she succeeded in making a stir: she must always be *en évidence*, so great was her thirst for notoriety. Madame de Boigne, who had known her well and recalled her with a vivid sense of regret, spoke of her in these exact words:

'Young women who lay themselves open to criticism are often very much to be pitied. Thrown suddenly in the vortex of worldly pleasures by their husbands, they do not always know how to command respect. Soon they become conspicuous through the instrumentality of those very ones who should be most interested in shielding them. Nine times out of ten this is the story of such poor neglected ones. I don't pretend to excuse the Princess Belgiojoso—her insatiable curiosity sometimes led her to overstep the bounds; but you may be certain that all the wrongs cannot be laid at her door.'

The reign of Louis Philippe was not conspicuous for a lofty ideal of social morality. Ridicule was openly and freely heaped upon the *bourgeois* virtues of the Court; but the world of fashion cannot be accused of prudery. Of ridicule, the Princess Belgiojoso came in for her fair share at the hands of Parisian wits, and few will deny that she deserved it; but of prudery she was guileless. The memoirs of her times, gossiping of her vagaries and eccentric adornment of house and person, of her encouragement of Thiers, de Musset, Heine, and others whose admiration and devotion she courted while repulsing their too passionate advances, tacitly absolve her from participation in the grosser forms of gallantry so dear to the corrupt society she frequented.

It was not, however, a lofty morality which protected her from the wilder ways of passion, but rather a temperamental indifference, partaking almost of the nature of a misfortune. Had her physical appetites been on a parity with her intellectual cravings, she would undoubtedly have rivalled her friend George Sand. As it was, however, a hypocritical and carping world, although it might jeer at or censure her haughtiness, could find no peg on which to hang an authenticated tale of misconduct or illicit sentimental adventure.

Great as the scandal was, few were astonished when Prince Belgiojoso suddenly fled with the beautiful young Duchess of Plaisance, a daughter of Berthier, Prince de Wagram, one of Napoleon's most famous henchmen. The fugitives took refuge in the Villa Pliniana on Lake Como, where, as related, Rossini had accomplished his *tour de force* during the composition of *Tancrede*. Here for eight years the guilty couple lay hidden, never once during that long period leaving the precincts of the park surrounding their gloomy abode.

Eventually the duchess was prevailed upon to leave her lover; but she settled in a villa on the opposite shore of the lake and stubbornly refused to return to France. She died in 1878, twenty years after the brilliant Prince Emilio, whose passionate devotion survived even the humiliation of her defection. A melancholy wanderer, without interests or pursuits, he led an aimless existence until disease overtook him and he passed away in the palace of his ancestors, at Milan, on February 17, 1858.

Outwardly the scandal of her husband's flight left Donna Christina unmoved. Her dignity, her sensitive pride, forbade any expression of concern. She was not misled by any desire to put her side of the story before the world, knowing full well that in any case the world will thrust its tongue in its cheek and believe just what it chooses. While the family of the duchess put their servants in deepest mourning and

Villa Pliniana on Lake Como

proclaimed the faithless wife and mother forever dead, the princess pursued the even tenor of her busy life undisturbed and, as far as the world knew, indifferent to the malicious slander to which the occurrence of necessity gave rise.

Chapter 5

Return to Paris

The next few years are full of strenuous endeavour to form and guide public opinion—especially in France—to an appreciation of the situation in Italy, and the wants and ideals of patriotic Italians. The Princess Belgiojoso was among the first to realise the incontrovertible fact that France alone was in a position to offer the moral encouragement and material aid indispensable for the social and political regeneration of Italy, of which axiom Cavour later became the great exponent.

The princess early became convinced of the inadequacy of the Mazzinian methods. Futile conspiracy and sporadic insurrection were in no way calculated to cope with the exigencies of a situation which demanded a careful preliminary manipulation of public opinion. Especially was this true in the case of Lombardy, where the zeal of the agitator was paralysed not only by a thoroughly organised and theoretically humane administration, but by the apathy of a populace to whom as yet the patriotic ideal conveyed so little. Official corruption such as existed in Naples and elsewhere was rare in the Italian provinces under Austrian rule.

Again, always excepting cases of political agitation, which were invariably classed with high treason and punished with barbaric severity, both the civil and military administrations were benign in comparison with those of some other Italian States. The princess (herself the recipient of the Imperial clemency through the restoration of her confiscated revenues) was fully aware that some greater incentive than an abstract principle was necessary to lift the dead weight of political apathy which crushed patriotism in the popular breast. The humiliation of his political nullity, and subjugation to the edicts emanating from the distant capital of a foreign conqueror, might rankle with the educated and ambitious Lombard or Venetian; but it was another matter to imbue the ignorant and careless proletariat with effective enthusiasm for an ideal the attainment of which guaranteed no definite relief from sordid material burdens.

Nevertheless, undaunted by the apparently insurmountable difficulties of the task, the princess threw herself heart and soul, body and mind, into the struggle. Her intellectual energies and those of the literary associates with whom she surrounded herself, as well as her fortune, were henceforth to be recklessly squandered upon the patriotic propaganda.

The *Speranze d'Italia* (1844) of Count Balbo had opened new channels of thought, fresh incentive to hope. The author appealed to the Italian princes to identify themselves with the national sentiment and join issue with their subjects in the liberation of Italy. With the founding of the *Gazzetta Italiana* (1845) the princess adopted and advocated the principles of Balbo, believing they provided a broad-minded solution calculated, at least theoretically, to reconcile the various conceptions of the patriotic ideal. Even Mazzini temporarily curbed the insurrectionary fervour of his pen to the composition of philosophical treatises on the problem of political education among Italians in various parts of the Peninsula.

Yet, despite the literary excellence of the *Gazzetta Italiana*, and the temperate, almost conciliatory, character of its critical essays, its sale was forbidden in Rome, Milan, Turin, and Florence. Dissensions arose between the brilliant writers on its staff, who chafed under the pretensions of its no less brilliant editor, founder, and financial supporter. For a time, the princess struggled on, carrying the entire editorial weight upon her frail shoulders, until financial complications compelled a temporary suspension of its publication.

In despair, the princess decided upon one of the boldest and most characteristic moves in her dramatic career. The Emperor Ferdinand I. had signalised his advent to the Austro-Hungarian throne in 1838 with the proclamation of a general amnesty for political offenders. The moment seemed propitious for reaping some advantage from this act of clemency, which at least accorded her facilities for revisiting her native city.

During the last days of December, 1845, the intrepid princess set out for Milan with no less an object in view than the flotation of shares in her patriotic but essentially anti-Austrian literary enterprise, thus audaciously carrying the war into the enemy's camp. Although the actual number of shares disposed of in Milan was disappointing from a financial point of view, (we only have record of some thirty-eight. Vieusseux correspondence in Royal National Library of Florence), the moral impetus given to the cause of Nationalism was not inconsiderable, while the personal prestige of the fearless champion of Liberty was greatly enhanced.

Strange to say, the Austrian authorities, although presumably aware of the subversive nature of the work the princess was so boldly engaged upon, and of her indefatigable efforts to enlist the suffrages of her fellow-citizens, yet shut their eyes and markedly ignored her propaganda. Did the governor, Count Spaur, hesitate to take advantage of the princess's apparently bold bid for martyrdom because he feared the inconvenient notoriety and comment her arrest could not fail to occasion, or did he seek subtly to discredit her prestige abroad by feigning to attach no real importance to the peevish intrigues of a notably eccentric woman, while at the same time prudently exercising a secret vigilance calculated effectively to neutralise any untoward demonstrations of popular sympathy? Be this as it may, the princess, on her side, refrained from an excess of zeal which she speedily realised would, under existing circumstances, be detrimental to her present aims.

With characteristic unexpectedness Donna Christina ostensibly withdrew from Milan. Retiring to her estate at Locate, situated within an hour's drive of the Capital, she threw herself with her usual wholeheartedness into schemes for the material and moral betterment of the peasantry, which eked out a precarious existence on the vast estates of the neighbourhood. Disconcerting as was the sudden change of front, the effacement of the ego political before the rural Lady Bountiful and agricultural economist, was as characteristic as had been the successive metamorphosis of the conspirator, the theologian and the *lionne* of the social salons of Paris. In nine cases, out of ten the intrinsic value of her political and literary achievement suffered owing to an invincible popular scepticism concerning her sincerity, provoked by her inconsistencies of conduct as well as by her erratic intellectual flights. The purely philanthropic nature of her present enthusiasm seemed beyond question.

The princess had been painfully impressed by the misery and want prevailing among the families of the field labourers, and had previously embodied her observations and suggestions for relief in a circular letter to the great landed proprietors of Lower Lombardy. (Copy pre-

Massimo D'Azeglio.

served in Museo del Risorgimento at Milan, No. 1353). But although the abstract principles underlying the crying social abuses which she revealed to her fellow-landowners must of necessity hold an important place in a mind as metaphysical, as analytical, and as mystical as that of Christina Belgiojoso, she now undertook the material improvement of her peasantry in a spirit of the most approved utilitarianism.

The ideal spiritual democracy which played so great a part in her dream of political regeneration sank into the background before the sordid reality of the economic problems at her door. Her ready sympathy was taxed to the utmost by daily contact with the misery, vice, and filth reaching to the very walls of her luxurious palace. By her order an apartment on the ground floor was fitted up as a recreation hall, and here, from dawn till midnight, some three hundred tired peasants found simple distraction and warmth. A refectory was added, where for a nominal price (in many cases gratis) nourishing soup could be obtained. Tasks suited to their limited capabilities, and at a fixed rate of remuneration, were provided for women and children, and later a glove factory was opened.

Primary and technical classes offered the children a means of redemption from the crass ignorance and moral degradation to which a poverty bestial in its attributes had relentlessly condemned them. The wretched hovels, lairs of a fever-stricken, grovelling population, were gradually replaced by humble, but decent and sanitary, abodes. Surely must the patient, downtrodden dolt, moulded during the centuries by the harsh egotism of his feudal lord, have risen up and called his princess blessed!

Ceaseless toil, and the continual drain upon the emotional depths of her supersensitive nature, soon began to tell upon the delicate constitution of Donna Christina. The distressing nervous disturbances to which she was a martyr assumed alarming proportions, the frequency of the attacks allowing of little time for recuperation. Urged by relatives and friends, the princess consulted Doctor Maspero, a clever physician, who promised her relief should she consent to place herself unreservedly in his hands. For several years Maspero never left his patient, devotedly following her on her various peregrinations. Although the princess rapidly improved under his care, the dire malady was never completely cured, and to its influences must be attributed many of the strange hallucinations and often wholly unaccountable extravagances of conduct which gave rise to so much malicious gossip. (Barbiera, *op. cit.*)

Having returned to Paris, and installed herself in her old quarters among familiar associations, Donna Christina was perforce drawn again into the intellectual vortex of the Capital. The activities seething in her brain demanded a medium of expression. The *Gazzetta Italiana*, rechristened the *Rivista Italian*, underwent radical metamorphosis, finally emerging under the classic title of *Ausonio*, (Ausonius, a Latin poet who lived about 310-394 *A.D*), and in form and volume resembling the then already famous *Revue des Deux Mondes*.

The purpose of this ambitious periodical was to familiarise not only Italians, but foreigners, and especially Frenchmen, with the social and moral conditions prevailing in Italy, and to enlist their sympathies with the awakening forces of Liberalism and the budding National sentiment, or what Italians call the "*Risorgimento*." Conceived in a literary spirit of the highest order, *Ausonio* opened its columns not only to dissertations on current politics, but devoted much space to the humanities and the *belles-lettres* of Romanticism. The eloquent pens of Manzoni and Massimo d'Azeglio, most classic in a generation of purists, were pressed into its service—the former protestingly, the latter with all the fire and fervour of an inspired prophet of Liberty, skilfully marshalling his serried ranks of fact and theory, and hurling his impassioned phrases with the resistless impetus of a cavalry charge.

The princess herself wrote at length and with many harrowing details of her recent experiences and experiments among her Italian tenants, endeavouring to excite the emulation of other great Lombard "slave-holders" in the moral and material emancipation she felt must precede the political regeneration of her countrymen.

Madame de Belgiojoso was not satisfied with the collaboration of her compatriots alone, distinguished as many of these writers were. She sought to press into her service French *littérateurs*; among others Arsène Houssaye, whom she summoned for a conference on this subject. Houssaye says:

> She wanted me to write in her already celebrated review *Ausonia*. She said to me, 'You are an Italian who has strayed north.' She wanted to prove to me that I was bound to devote myself body and soul to the Latin races. She still cherished the beatific illusion that the Pope was on her side. 'There is no doubt but that we shall soon hear of doings on the other side of the Alps,' she said.
>
> 'Yes, Princess,' I replied, 'but the Pope won't have any hand in

VINCENZO GIOBERT.

them, for the very reason that he *is* Pope, and that the strength of the Papacy lies in silence.' She then continued: 'The Italians of today don't forget that their ancestors were Romans: at Brescia the commander of the town—a merciless Austrian—boasted loudly in a café that in Vienna a man's head was worth five florins; "In Milan," he added contemptuously, "it isn't worth more than five pence." He was killed by the people,' finished the princess, 'who cried as he fell, "Here it is worth nothing at all."'—*Les Confessions*, vol. ii.

From 1840 to 1846 the political stagnation of Italy was complete. Austrian influence reigned supreme from Venice to Naples. In Piedmont, the Jesuits still retained their grip over the mind of the irresolute Charles Albert, whom Constitutionalists in exile berated or flattered in vain. Mazzini, from his refuge in Switzerland or England, passionately exhorted his followers to revolt, and by means of pamphlets, smuggled at the risk of life or liberty, sought to fire the imagination of the only too inflammable youth of Lombardy-Venetia. (Cadolini's curious article in *Nuova Antologia*, February 16, 1905.)

To cooler heads the forcible expulsion of Austria seemed Utopian: the great mass of educated Italians, who had too much common-sense or too little courage for Mazzini's gospel, were looking for a milder creed which would reconcile patriotism and prudence. The pathetic tragedy of the Bandiera brothers, two hot-headed young Mazzinians who in 1844, together with a handful of companions, hurled themselves against the rock of Neapolitan Absolutism, and were shattered in the vain attempt, discredited the irresponsible agitator to whose influence the mad venture was due. Where political revolutions are concerned failure is equivalent to a principle violated: success alone can excuse tampering with the constituted social organisation of the State.

Thinking patriots decried the petty plots and sporadic risings which served no useful purpose, merely embittering the despotism they sought to destroy. To many of these, men noted for physical as well as moral courage, the "milder creed" presented practical eventualities which under existing circumstances the revolution with fire and sword would be powerless to achieve. With the Princess Belgiojoso, they relied for the creation of an atmosphere in which despotism could not live, on the introduction of agricultural reform, savings banks, schools, the promotion of literary journals and of scientific societies, and the building of railways.

Progress, the steady advance of social and material civilisation in Italy, combined with the diffusion abroad of an accurate knowledge of the aims and legitimate aspirations of those engaged in the struggle for national regeneration, was the refrain *Ausonio* dinned into the ears of its readers. But the circulation of *Ausonio* was never considerable, while its authority was contested and its teachings ridiculed by many who looked upon the princess as an irresponsible and hysterical visionary.

A man arose, however, whose genius commanded a hearing for Italy and her woes. Gioberti, at once a priest and a Liberal, whose politics had made him a victim of the ferocious repressive measures instigated during the opening years of Charles Albert's reign, captivated intellectual France no less than Italy with his *Moral and Civil Primacy of the Italians* (1843). The transcendentalism of his philosophy, while it appealed irresistibly to the religious and aristocratic side of the princess's patriotism, failed to satisfy her conception of the virility of a politically reconstructed Italy.

A modern Italy based on the ascendency of the past could not but attract the daughter of the proud House of Trivulzio. Donna Christina, despite her vaunted Republicanism, never abandoned her allegiance to the monarchical principle. Yet, her practical common sense accepted with scepticism the theory that a Pope could or would ever lead the cause of Nationality and reform. Doubtless she and many others were prepared on the accession of Pius IX. to retract or modify the convictions of three years before; but the period of uncertainty was brief, and the fallacy of Gioberti's rhetoric soon apparent. (Leone Carpi, in his *Risorgimento Italiano*, vol. i., speaks of an insult offered the Princess Belgiojoso in one of Gioberti's works, "fortunately forgotten.")

In strong contrast to the optimism of Gioberti's philosophical theorising came d'Azeglio's *Ultimi Cast di Romagna* (1845), which exposed to the world, in measured but forcible language, the terrorism exercised in the name of the Pope (Gregory XVI.) at Ravenna and Rimini. It was a "scathing commentary on the dream of a regenerating Papacy," and Europe stood aghast at the ferocity displayed by the Vicar of Christ. The revolt of the Liberals in Romagna had not been directed against the person of their temporal and spiritual sovereign. The insurgents demanded the reform of a corrupt hierarchical administration and its attendant intolerable abuses, to which they called "the Princes and Peoples of Europe" as witness. But Austria sided with the

Papal policy, and hounded the disbanded Liberals while the various European chancelleries stood aloof.

Italian patriotism as represented by the more thoughtful elements became increasingly convinced not only of the futility but of the mischievous nature of the Mazzinian type of conspiracy and petty revolt. If Republicanism was discredited, it was in no small measure due to the inflexibility, the uncompromising narrowness of Mazzini's methods, which made no allowance for prejudice or tradition, and invariably tended to extremes. The moderation of the political creed preached by d'Azeglio, and his political suggestions for the utilisation of material at hand, was of incalculable value, turning, as it did, the tide of nationalist sentiment once more in the direction of Piedmont.

But new and irresistible forces were at work, the revolutionising powers of which were as yet suspected only by the few. Count Cavour entered upon his marvellous career with a strenuous and convincing programme which embraced agricultural reforms, industrial expansion and the introduction of railway communication with neighbouring Italian States. Only by frequent and ready intercourse, and the community of social and commercial interest thus created, he argued, could a satisfactory reciprocal political solidarity be attained.

Charles Albert himself was gradually but surely drawn into the current. Of enthusiasm or initiative, he had none: even the ambition implied by his subsequent actions lacked spontaneity, being the impersonal result of a relentless rush of circumstance. His hatred of Austria, however, was genuine. Veiled and timid of expression as the sentiment was towards the nation which had humiliated him in his youth, sought to filch his crown, and even yet pretended to a moral censorship over his domestic and foreign policy, the king's resentment grew bolder with the spread of his popularity at home. No thoroughly satisfactory analysis of the character of this royal sphinx exists. He was a victim of circumstances in the net of which his own hesitating, weak and shifting nature had largely contributed towards entangling him.

As reported in his own words, he stood "between the poisoned chocolate of the Jesuits (the masters of his political as of his spiritual conscience) and the dagger of the Carbonari" (or the consequences of his early association with the party of emancipation and reform). That by his own volition he would ever have shaken himself free of the trammels of the reactionary Clericals is problematical: the mysticism of his nature craved spiritual support and shrank with abhorrence from the materialism he was taught to believe lurked beneath the principles professed by Liberals and Nationalists. But his hand was forced.

The election of Pius IX. revolutionised Italian political conceptions (June, 1846). As cardinal, he had professed himself in sympathy with the tenets and aspirations not only of the Liberals but of the Nationalists to boot. A Liberal Pope! Were the rhetorical effusions of the ex-priest Gioberti destined to assume shape and substance? Were liberty and independence to be achieved by means of this new standard of traditional and reactionary Conservatism? All Italy was in a ferment of jubilation or dismay. The people cheered, the rulers groaned. Expectation loomed large; while the anti-Austrian sentiment grew restless and impatient of delay. Hurried from one concession to another, without power to stem the flood his Platonic sympathies had set free, Pius still hesitated at the final plunge, realising that the grant of representative institutions must weaken, if not eventually destroy, the prestige of Theocracy.

In Naples, the pressure became so strong that the perjured Ferdinand II. yielded to the popular demand; thus, inaugurating the era of constitutional reform in Italy.

Brushing aside any scruples of conscience he may still have entertained, Charles Albert a week later (February, 1848) promised his subjects the grant of a charter—a political covenant which, unlike the ephemeral pacts of half the States of modern Europe, was destined to live and flourish.

CHAPTER 6

The Princess and Louis Napoleon

Meanwhile the Princess Belgiojoso, a close student of French public affairs, became more and more convinced that the France of Louis Philippe would never afford aid to Italy in the inevitable struggle with Austria. The old king sought to make his peace with his fellow-sovereigns, who had looked with horror on what they stigmatised his usurpation. A revolutionary wave had carried him to his exalted position, but the receding ebb gradually isolated him, until another and mightier tide swept him to destruction. In his egotism this "King of the Barricades," child of the Revolution though he was, forgetful of his origin, turned from Liberalism and deliberately courted that incarnation of Absolutism, Prince Metternich, Chancellor of the Austrian Empire.

Instinctively Christina Belgiojoso anticipated the collapse of a ré-gime which, although founded on and owing its very existence to the democratic principle, offered hostages to the partisans of reaction. The closer his relations with the power representing and professing the doctrines of Absolutism, the more Louis Philippe saw himself constrained to approximate to their system, and consequently to estrange himself from the spirit, when not the letter, of Constitutionalism. France smarted under the humiliations of the Treaty of Vienna (1815). As Lamartine said, the country "needed air" and freedom of action; yet her "Citizen King" allowed himself to be drawn into the orbit of the reactionary influences which sought to smother her ambitions and paralyse national initiative.

Although the chances for a revival of Bonapartism seemed particularly remote with the fiasco at Strasburg (1836) and the hardly less humiliating failure at Boulogne still fresh in men's minds, an infinitesimal minority maintained that Prince Louis Napoleon alone offered guarantees for the revival of the national prestige abroad, in conjunction with a conscientious interpretation of popular liberty at home. In the person of the nephew of the Liberator of Italy, Christina recognised a fellow-conspirator and a sympathetic supporter of the cause she had so greatly at heart. Louis Napoleon had in early youth been affiliated with the Carbonari, and had fought against the Papal forces during the insurrection of 1831. Perhaps as one of the initiated the princess was aware of the nature of the secret links which bound the ex-Carbonaro to certain political factions of a later date, links which are believed to have occasionally been the cause of considerable embarrassment to the Emperor of the French. Louis Philippe had banished the author of the Strasburg plot to America; the disturber of the public peace at Boulogne he confined in the fortress of Ham.

After his sensational escape from prison (1846) and flight to England, the Princess Belgiojoso lost no time in seeking out the Pretender and laying before him her schemes and aspirations.

The meeting took place in London in the spring of 1846, Doctor Maspero assisting at the somewhat emotional interview, during which not only the affairs of Italy but the significant drift of French politics were freely discussed. Her extended and varied relations with French statesmen and politicians of all shades of opinion, together with her intimate connections in the Parisian social world for the past sixteen years, lent to the princess's deductions a weight not lightly to be ignored. Allowance being made for characteristic impulsiveness, the information she possessed was reliable, and her personal views of the political outlook were based on sound and rational premises.

At the conclusion of the interview the ambitious exile, whose opportunity was now so near, grasping the hands of his eloquent interlocutor, exclaimed with unusual warmth:

Princess, let me first arrange matters in France, then I will think of Italy.

Two years later Louis Philippe sought refuge on British soil (February, 1848), and France acclaimed the Republic which served Louis Napoleon as a stepping-stone to Empire.

For the Princess Belgiojoso the two years following her visit to London were full of intellectual activity. Precursors of the coming storm which was to revolutionise Europe were manifest on all sides: especially in Italy was the unrest apparent. In Lombardy, the hopes raised by the accession of Pius IX. rekindled the fires of patriotism, and the tension became perilously strained. Milan seethed and surged in sullen protest under old Radetzky's contemptuous provocations.

The Austrians were boycotted in high society, and not even an archduke could find an Italian partner at a ball. The spirit of defiance was abroad: it permeated all social ranks, from the aristocrat in his palace to the artisan; even the peasant in the rice-fields and the shepherd on the mountain slopes caught the infection. Any pretext for an anti-Austrian demonstration was eagerly seized. The funeral of Count Confalonieri (whose conspiracies, arrest and trial, have been mentioned in these pages) gave rise to imposing manifestations of popular sympathy with the patriot whom long martyrdom had invested with the dignity of a national hero.

By some the Princess Belgiojoso has been held indirectly responsible for the death of Confalonieri. (Barbiera, *op. cit.* D'Ancona, in his *Federico Confalonieri* makes no mention of Princess Belgiojoso's pamphlet.) The publication of her pamphlet *Studies of the History of Lombardy during Recent Years*, (1846), so angered the proud and intolerant count, who brooked no criticism, that he left Paris for Milan in the heart of winter. Broken in health by his long confinement in the dungeons of the Spielberg, and suffering moreover from dropsy, Confalonieri expired at Hospenthal, near the summit of the St. Gotthard, on December 10, 1846.

It will be remembered that the Marquis d'Aragona, stepfather of Donna Christina, was implicated in the famous trial, narrowly escaping the fate which befell his fellow-conspirators. The able defence undertaken in his behalf by Professor d'Ancona, (*Federico Confalonieri*), would seem to exculpate Confalonieri from most of the accusations brought against him; but his overbearing, haughty character made him many enemies, while an unfortunate propensity for exciting malicious discord among mutual friends still further reduced the sympathy to which his sufferings in a patriotic cause entitled him. Confalonieri living had been a thorn in the side of Austria; his funeral, with the audaciously expressed patriotic manifestations to which it gave rise, added to the growing embarrassments of the Imperial authorities.

Yet while it would be manifestly unfair to belittle the ceaseless efforts of intelligent and devoted patriots who sought to awaken national enthusiasm by means of the example of individual sacrifice, or through an educational campaign of political literature, the Cavourian theory of moral advance through material progression, based on mutual interest, was perhaps, as potent a factor in the formation of a public spirit among the masses as any of the ethical considerations propagated by the doctrinaires. Paradoxical as it must appear, the very quarrels and disputes between rival towns and communes concerning the lines of the projected railways, led to the political solidarity of a later day. An appreciation of mutual material interests was followed by the disclosure of the identity of popular political aspirations towards Nationalism.

The tariff war of 1846 committed Charles Albert to a policy of commercial antagonism towards Austria to which the peculiarly intimate social bonds existing between Piedmont and those portions of Lombardy bordering on the frontier, added a political significance. The conviction gained ground in the provinces under Austrian rule that Charles Albert was neither disinclined nor unprepared to join issues with Lombardy against a common foe.

The visible unrest and openly expressed criticism warned Austria of the approaching storm. As a conciliatory measure perhaps, it was decreed in Vienna that the successor of the recently deceased Archbishop of Milan should be an Italian. The appointment was greeted with an outburst of popular enthusiasm well-nigh delirious in its intensity.

That the Nationalists seized upon the concession for the manufacture of political capital is probable. But the undue prolongation of patriotic demonstrations angered the overweening Radetzky, whose troops resorted to violence and bloodshed in quelling the outwardly pacific if covertly subversive rejoicings (September, 1847). "Three days of blood will give us thirty years of peace," the autocratic old commander-in-chief, is reported to have cynically remarked when remonstrated with for the gratuitous brutality of his methods.

But the temper of the masses had been aroused. Sullen, still cringing before their oppressors, they secretly prepared their revenge for the unjustifiable insults to which they were subjected by Radetzky, now anxious to provoke open revolt. The so-called Tobacco Riots furnished the desired pretext. As a protest against the unwarranted severity of their tyrants an edict went forth among Milanese patriots suspending the use of tobacco on and after January 1, 1848. New Year's Day found the streets of Milan practically smokeless, the few who ventured abroad with the hitherto ubiquitous cigar being speedily prevailed on to obey the popular decree.

The demonstration, with its avowed object of aiming a blow against the fiscal revenues of the Empire, maddened Radetzky. Austrian offic-

BUILDING A BARRICADE MILAN

ers and soldiers, liberally provided with cigars, took possession of the streets, puffing smoke in the faces of the abstemious citizens. When the outrage was resented and riots took place, the cavalry charged the unarmed crowds, killing several and wounding more. The disturbances spread to Bergamo, Verona, Brescia, and other cities, whose citizens had imitated Milan, and renounced tobacco with a like motive.

Milan was quickly brought into sullen subjection, but Italy took fire from the sparks of the Austrian cigars so freely consumed on the streets of the Lombard capital on this memorable occasion. In Tuscany, in Naples, in Venetia, a hundred meetings clamoured for the expulsion of the foreigner and the proclamation of constitutional liberties and political reform.

On March 17, 1848, stupendous tidings reached Milan. Hungary was in rebellion, Vienna in the hands of the Constitutionalists; the hated Metternich had fallen. The potentialities of the situation, rendered even more favourable by the overthrow of Louis Philippe and the establishment of a Republic in France, were manifest. Milan realised that her hour of vengeance was at hand.

As if by magic, hundreds of barricades bristled in the path of the Austrian regulars. Furniture, pictures, beds and mattresses, pianos, and the benches torn from neighbouring churches, formed the material with which the flimsy defences were constructed. Radetzky disposed of some twenty thousand troops, well-armed, trained and disciplined. At the outset, the insurrectionists had little more than such primitive missiles as stones, tiles, and empty bottles to oppose to the rifles of the Tyrolese sharpshooters and the cannon of the artillerymen. Men, women, and children, mad with frenzied enthusiasm, tore up the pavements, stripped the roofs of tiles, hurling everything that came to hand upon their foes. From the windows in the narrow streets boiling oil or water was freely emptied on the heads of the troops.

The Moravian, Bohemian, and Croatian soldiery committed atrocities which lashed the blood of the insurgents to fever heat. Radetzky urged his men to grant no quarter, and even prisoners were massacred in cold blood. Both sides committed excesses, but again many acts of sublime forbearance are recorded.

George Sand relates an episode, (*Souvenirs et Idées*), vouched for by Mazzini himself, which is in strong contrast to the brutality of Radetzky's procedure. In one of the beleaguered barracks several of the starving Austrians piteously begged their besiegers for bread. A youth of sixteen fearlessly approached the wall, and affixing a loaf to his bayonet, passed it over to the famished men. At the same moment, a shot was fired from within, and the boy dropped dead. A few hours later the barracks were carried by storm, and the infuriated populace demanded that the murderer of the boy be delivered up. To save their own lives the miserable soldiery pointed to one of their comrades who lay terribly wounded at their feet. But at the sight of his helplessness and suffering the wrath of the people was turned to pity and the wretched miscreant was tenderly cared for.

Among the first to hasten to the aid of his fellow-citizens was the Marquis Pallavicino, whose ten years' martyrdom in Austrian dungeons as a consequence of his participation in the conspiracies of 1821, had in nowise diminished his patriotic ardour. Armed with an old shot-gun and accompanied by his brother-in-law, Count Louis Belgiojoso, a cousin of the Princess Christina, the ex-Carbonaro besought his companions to see to it that should he be wounded he did not fall into the hands of their enemy alive, says he, (*Memorie*, vol. i.):

During these terrible moments, I had ever before me a mental picture of the Spielberg, with all its untold sufferings.

Physical courage was not the only virtue displayed by the heroic population during the glorious "Five Days." The milk of human kindness flowed as freely as blood. Rich and poor, noble and plebeian, stood shoulder to shoulder behind the barricades. The palaces of the great aristocrats were thrown open, offering shelter and refreshment to all classes: caste prejudices melted in the face of a common aim, and "Milan for five days offered to the world a spectacle worthy of the angels, but too transcendental for mortal man." (*Op. cit.*) Hidden in a stack of hay, Count Bolza, the execrated chief of secret police, was discovered and dragged forth by a mob threatening dire reprisals.

"If you kill him," shouted Cattaneo, " you accomplish an act of justice; if you grant him his life, your action is a holy one."

And the mob surrendered its prey.

Count Hübner, an emissary of Metternich and later Austrian Ambassador in Paris, has left a thrilling narration of the weeks he spent in hiding in Milan during the insurrection. To the humanity displayed by the victorious mob he too pays eloquent tribute. When the Royal Palace fell into the hands of the insurgents its terrified inmates were treated almost with consideration.

There was no pillage—a fact which merits recording. Our soldiers (the Austrians) posted at the windows of the palace and on the roof of the cathedral had during the previous two days killed a considerable number of insurgents. Now, free to wreak their vengeance, intoxicated by success, these people, for the most part belonging to the lower classes, sacked the palace, it is true, during the first flush of their exultation, but harmed neither the persons nor the property of the vanquished.—*Une Année de ma vie.*

Step by step, street by street, the victorious insurgents drove their famished and demoralised foe before them. Radetzky proposed an armistice, but the Municipal Council, which had assumed the functions of a Provisional Government, would listen to nothing short of immediate and unconditional evacuation. On the 22nd the Austrians, realising the hopelessness of the situation with starvation staring them in the face, abandoned the castle and the few positions remaining to them, and evacuated the city. Milan echoed with enthusiastic cries of "*Viva Pio Nono!*" "*Viva l'Italia!*" or "*Viva l'Indipendenza!*"

Yet precisely what form this dearly purchased independence was to assume, not a dozen of the heroic patriots who had dislodged and routed an army were prepared to decide. To the majority it was all-sufficient that the hated white uniform of the Austrian, stained with blood and besmeared with the mud of defeat, had disappeared from their city. True, Charles Albert had been appealed to on the outbreak of the insurrection, but as was his wont the king had given equivocal assurances of assistance. It was only when assured that the movement was not Republican in its aspirations, but really imbued with the Nationalist spirit which had ever looked to him as its natural champion, that the ruler of Piedmont issued a proclamation to the Peoples of Lombardy and Venetia, followed by a declaration of war on Austria (March 25, 1848).

CHAPTER 7

Her Entry into Milan

Three months prior to the events related in the last chapter, Ferdinand II. of Naples had thrown wide the portals of Hope by the grant of constitutional liberties to his subjects.

Christina Belgiojoso followed the vanguard of political exiles who availed themselves of the amnesty to offer their services to a government, apparently now converted to the principles of liberty and equity, for which they had sacrificed the best years of their lives. Although the princess could not herself aspire to direct participation in the administration of public affairs, her deep interest in social and political reform, and her personal influence with several of the most distinguished Southern patriots, decided her presence in Naples.

It was in the Bourbon capital, therefore, that news of the amazing events in Milan surprised her. With characteristic promptitude she chartered a steamer to convey her to Genoa, whence she could more rapidly proceed to the scene of action. No sooner had the rumour of her imminent departure become bruited through the city than she found herself besieged by patriots of all social grades, clamouring for permission to accompany her.

It is well-nigh impossible to disentangle the threads of such circumstantial evidence as we possess concerning the original motive which prompted the princess to secure this costly means of rapid transport to Milan. There is valid reason for the belief, however, that the revolutionary enthusiast never intended the vessel for her own private and exclusive conveyance. It is much more probable that the sensational project of an armed expedition germed in her fertile brain with the earliest tidings of the successful rising, and the certainty that Piedmont must become officially involved in the struggle to cast off the foreign yoke.

Knowing the princess's love of sensational effect, we can readily appreciate how this opportunity of playing the role of a modern Joan of Arc must have appealed to her. Although she could hardly issue a call for volunteers on an expedition directed against a government with which the Neapolitan sovereign was at peace, the peculiar political conditions of the moment made it tolerably sure that the local authorities would be conveniently blind to the filibustering character of the escapade. And so, it proved. King "Bomba," who, despite his newly fledged Constitutionalism, concealed with difficulty his undying hatred of the Liberals, must have writhed in impotent rage while following with the tail of his eye the launching of an expedition which the insecurity of his own throne alone prevented his frustrating.

In an article published in the *Revue des Deux Mondes*, entitled "*L'Italic et la Revolution Italienne*," (October 1, 1848), the Princess Belgiojoso furnishes us with many curious details of this most sensational episode of her eventful career. The strange and challenging personality of the heroine is brought conspicuously before the reader, who hesitates whether to smile at the incongruity of the picture presented by this frail and sickly intellectualist, surrounded by a heterogeneous horde of raw enthusiasts, or endorse with sincere admiration the real nobility of purpose underlying the theatrical aspect of the fantastic pageant.

Princess Belgiojoso thus picturesquely describes the stirring scenes attending her departure from Naples:—

Hardly had the news of my project become noised abroad than I had occasion to learn how great and fervent was the sympathy which the Lombard cause excited in Naples. Volunteers of all social grades came to beg me to conduct them to Lombardy. During the forty-eight hours which preceded my sailing my house was never empty; ten thousand Neapolitans were ready to follow me; but my steamer could carry but two hundred passengers. I consented, therefore, to accept that number, and the little column was instantly completed.

Rarely has a whole population been seen to awake unexpectedly from a long lethargy, aroused by the sole incentives of war and devotion. Among the volunteers who craved following me to Lombardy some belonged to the highest society of Naples: abandoning by stealth the paternal roof, they insisted on accompanying me, carrying in their pockets but a few coins. Oth-

PRINCESS BELGIOJOSO AND A VOLUNTEER

ers, employees in modest circumstances, exchanged without regret the positions on which they depended for a livelihood for the hardships of camp life.

Several officers risked the punishment meted out to deserters in order to bear arms against Austria: many fathers of families left behind them wife and children; and one young man, whose long-awaited marriage was to have been celebrated on the morrow, postponed his dearest hopes in his eagerness to defend his country. Never shall I forget the moment of my departure. The day was glorious. We were to embark that evening at five. When I reached the steamer the sea was covered with little boats which had put out from all directions to wish us God-speed.

Our vessel was readily distinguishable from the many others at anchor in the port by the shimmer of the arms piled on its decks. My volunteers awaited me. During the short delay occasioned by the last preparations we were assailed by innumerable supplicants: from all the skiffs surrounding our steamer arose voices of entreaty urging us to inscribe one more name on the already overflowing list. We could, unfortunately, but reiteratedly refuse these inopportune appeals, and when our steamer cast off, one single shout went up from a hundred thousand mouths, speeding us with these words: 'We shall follow you!'—

(The responsibility for these figures rests with the princess.

Fortunately, the sea was calm and the voyage uneventful. Of military discipline, there was no pretence.

Alone amidst the turbulent throng, this fragile woman, not yet forty years of age and still marvellously beautiful, ruled supreme by virtue of a patriotic exaltation, which enshrined her in the hearts of her followers as a being apart—a goddess of Liberty—inviolate, sacred. The cause she championed was a holy one. Like some knight crusader of old, this descendant of a warlike race wielded despotic authority over her motley band. She distributed brevets of rank to her battalion, the curious commissions reading, "We, Princess Christina di Belgiojoso, do hereby name and appoint," &c., &c. That this action excited no ridicule will convey some idea of the intensity of the passionate and romantic fervour which reigned among her followers, who unhesitatingly placed their destinies in her eccentric keeping.

The princess joined in the universal cry of "*Viva l'Italia!*" "*Viva Pio*

Nono!" "*Viva l'Indipendenza!*" and that she did so in all sincerity we do not question. Whatever scepticism she may have entertained concerning the supremacy of a theocratic government in a politically and nationally regenerated Italy was buried deep until the all-important task of effectually and permanently expelling the hated foreigner should be accomplished. Nevertheless, for one reason or another, the impression prevailing with the Provisional Government at Milan would seem to have been that the princess's volunteers were distinctly Republican in their sympathies and aspirations, and, as a consequence, their arrival caused considerable embarrassment in official circles.

The princess herself writes:

> The population of Milan prepared to salute our arrival with marks of sympathy, with which the Provisional Government judged prudent to associate itself. My two hundred volunteers were, after the Piedmontese, the first Italians who came to Lombardy to take part in what was then styled the 'Crusade' and the 'Holy War.' The presence in Milan of the first corps of Neapolitan volunteers seemed to warrant the belief that the war against Austria would become an Italian, rather than a Lombard-Piedmontese, war. The consecutive departures of four other Neapolitan legions soon added to the feeling of confidence which the arrival of the first volunteers had already inspired. Several of our authorities, however, refused to share this confidence.

First and foremost among those who looked askance at the "troop of adventurers" which the princess brought in her train was Count Casati, who had been elected President of the Provisional Government, and whose administration Donna Christina later so severely criticised. Truth to tell, the Neapolitan volunteers were not received with feelings of unmixed joy. In official circles, the princess met with undisguised ill-will when endeavouring to interest the government in her battalion. When she represented her volunteers as "the advance guard of an army a hundred thousand strong, composed of the flower of Italian youth," only awaiting a signal to press forward, she was met with cries of "God preserve us from such aid!" uttered by a government aghast at the possibility of a like invasion.

Count Hübner was an eye-witness of the entry of the *bizarre* throng which swarmed into Milan at the heels of its fantastic leader. On his return from Brescia, whither he had gone on a fruitless mission concerning an exchange of prisoners, or hostages, as it was preferred to call them, he found Milan in a state of jubilation. A fear seized upon the Austrian lest the explanation be found in the receipt of news of some signal victory over Marshal Radetzky, who after the evacuation of Milan had fallen back on Verona. He soon learnt the reason of the hubbub, which was caused by the entry of the Neapolitan volunteers with the Princess Belgiojoso leading the procession. Hübner writes:

> Our carriage was stopped during the march past, and I was enabled to contemplate at my ease the heroine of the day, whom I had formerly frequently met in Paris *salons*. The last ten years had not passed over her head without leaving their traces, but she was still a beautiful woman. Followed by her *giovinotti napolitani*, she carried a large flag, (see frontispiece), composed of the Italian colours, (red, white, and green). From the windows and balconies innumerable handkerchiefs waved, and the air resounded with applause of the public.—Hübner, *op. cit.*

On her arrival in the square before the church of San Fedele, Count Casati received the princess with a most eloquent speech. We know that the President of the Provisional Government did not share the popular enthusiasm the advent of the eccentric patriot and her hot-headed contingent had aroused. He wrote privately to a friend:

> I fear she has made me an awkward present. Nevertheless, I had to figure in the scene, and to harangue the troops. (Letter cited by Barbiera, *op. cit.*)

Hübner continues:

> A few days later, these budding young heroes, after having been feasted at the expense of the town, were put on the train at the Porta Tosca station and despatched to the seat of war. Three weeks later (as I write these lines) a score of poor devils in rags can be seen begging alms in the streets of Milan. This is all that remains of the Neapolitan braves. They never saw the enemy, but committed such depredations of all kinds that the exasperated peasantry more or less exterminated them. Thus, ended this great and essentially Republican demonstration. The government at the Palazzo Marino, which is not Republican, laughs in its sleeve: The princess, I doubt not, will easily console herself, and will find means of occupying her leisure: the Milanese had their three or four days of show and patriotic fuss

gratis. Everybody ought consequently to be satisfied, except the unfortunate Neapolitan *giovanotti* (youths).—Hübner, *op. cit.*

This cynical conclusion is perhaps exaggerated; but there is reason to believe that the dissolution of the Neapolitan contingent, numerically insignificant, yet suspected of inconvenient political leanings which might influence the populace, came as a relief to the government which had offered pledges to Charles Albert and the political system he represented. The Austrian diplomatist knew his Italy well. His diagnosis of the internal forces at work, his appreciation of their significance, strength and weakness, is consummate, penetrating, and in the main fair. Frankly recognising and deploring the faults committed in Vienna in the administration of the Italian provinces, his comments on the political phenomena which came under his personal observation during the hundred and six days of his captivity in Milan—a hostage in the hands of the Provisional Government—are imbued with a rare moderation.

By a strange irony of fate, it was to this same impassive diplomat, when ten years later he served his country as ambassador in Paris, that the Emperor Napoleon III. uttered the enigmatic words which were to find echo at Magenta and Solferino a few months after. Napoleon said to the imperturbable ambassador:

> I regret, that our relations are not as friendly as I should desire, but I beg you to write to Vienna that my personal sentiments towards the emperor are unchanged.—Despatch of Hübner to Buol, January 1, 1859.

Mazzini arrived in Milan on April 7th. Although the Princess Belgiojoso had virtually repudiated the uncompromising creed of the Republican agitator, and ostensibly pinned her faith to the House of Savoy as the regenerating medium of her country, her apostasy was not generally accepted as final. An ambiguous disclaimer in her letter to Charles Albert (April 13, 1848) failed to convince the Piedmontese authorities of the sincerity of her enthusiasm, she wrote:

> My sympathies are not with the Republic, but with the individuals who compose the Republican party.

The distinction was too subtle to inspire confidence. Hence the small influence possessed by the princess with the more practical members of the Provisional Government, to whose uncertain guidance the destinies of the imperfectly emancipated province were entrusted. They dared not openly snub Mazzini, but they did little to propitiate the heroine of the quickly discredited Neapolitan invasion.

The princess relates that the reception accorded Mazzini by the Milanese authorities was brilliant and flattering. (*Revue des Deux Mondes*, September 15, 1848.) The representatives of both factions, Monarchical and Republican, vied with each other in bidding for his suffrage.

> The Royalists hoped to win him over to their constitutional aspirations: The Republicans illuded themselves with the confidence that Mazzini's eloquence must either convert their colleagues, or, failing this, that by bringing them into close relations with the chief of the Republican faction they might become compromised in the eyes of Charles Albert.

Discord soon resulted, as was indeed inevitable when members of the same revolutionary *Junta* held such widely divergent theories concerning not merely the form of government to be adopted, but also as to the means by which their temporary victory over Austria was to be substantiated and independence permanently guaranteed. Even the most sanguine realised that their unaided efforts must, in the open field, prove futile when pitted against the trained and reinforced legions of Radetzky. The support of France was more than dubious, and little efficient aid could be expected from any of the native States of the Peninsula, with the sole exception of Piedmont.

Mazzini himself, distasteful as was the truth that independence could be achieved only under the banner of a Royal House, did not maintain his opposition to the political union of Lombardy with Piedmont. He *did* insist, however, that certain guarantees should be exacted establishing the right of the Lombards on the termination of the war to decide their own political destiny, irrespective of the claims and interests of a dynasty which, he urged, must be unhesitatingly sacrificed to the common weal.

Any concession was significant coming from so rabid an extremist who, theoretically, refused to credit salvation on lines other than the obliteration of the past and the reconstruction of the State on a fundamental basis of popular liberties owing nothing to the era whose destruction they compassed. Yet the union of Lombardy and Venetia under the sceptre of the House of Savoy, unpalatable though it was, could, in the estimation of the great visionary, but slightly delay the irresistible onward march of the principles of social freedom of which he was the prophet.

That the Princess Belgiojoso was fully alive to the gravity of the crisis is demonstrated by her remarkable literary output at this period. Not content with frequent contributions to the French political press—principally to the *Constitutionnel, Démocratic pacifique*, and *National*, she founded and edited two journals in Milan: *Il Crociato* (*The Crusader*) and *La Croce di Savoia* (*Cross of Savoy*). In addition to the labours attending on the publication of these papers, and to her voluminous private correspondence, her indefatigable mental activity sought distraction in the compilation of political pamphlets, and even aspired to the formation and personal leadership of a political party frankly in accord with the Unitarian ambitions of Charles Albert.

None of her writings, however, afford a clearer conception of the exaltation of the phase through which she was passing than the letter addressed by the princess to the King of Sardinia. It is at once a profession of faith, a petition, and a menace. The vanity of the *femme politique*, the flame of whose megalomania has been fanned by the sycophants of the literary salon, is naively to the fore: yet the sound common sense of her argument, the accuracy and political acumen displayed in her appreciation and elucidation of the impending crisis, its possibilities and probabilities, rank the curious document with those of practical value to the historian.

The letter is dated April 13, 1848, and was written from the princess's temporary retreat at the little village of Belgiojoso, within easy driving distance of Milan:—

Sire

May your Majesty forgive the candid language of a person unused to the formalities of a Court, and accustomed to express without veil or reticence her personal opinions. Your Majesty is aware how ardently I have desired your intervention in Lombardy. Unfortunately, my fervent prayers were tardily granted, when the Milanese believed they had accomplished unaided the most arduous part of the undertaking. This delay now renders dubious what would have been certain had your Majesty crossed the Ticino a few days before the insurrection in Milan. My opinion is unchanged: I desire with all my heart the union of Lombardy with Piedmont, and I am commissioned by influential persons in Naples to effect a coalition between the Piedmontese party in Naples and the partisans of Piedmont in

Lombardy. The fate of Italy hangs on the decision adopted by the Lombards.

Either we unite with Piedmont, and, perhaps before two years are past, all Italy will be gathered under the House of Savoy, or we proclaim ourselves a Republic, and, Genoa imitating us, the military strength of Piedmont is reduced to insignificance; Italy becomes subdivided into numberless States, and we return to the Middle Ages. Your Majesty can readily understand how greatly I desire the first of these solutions. I received this morning an urgent appeal from the representative of a strong and friendly Power to place myself at the head of the party of union with Piedmont.

To this person I made the following objections, which your Majesty, should you be willing, can remove. Two parties at present face each other in Milan, the Piedmontese and the Republican: the Piedmontese is composed of the Milanese aristocracy that is to say, of those who, a year ago, were the friends of Austria; of the Provincial Government; and of those persons who are prompted by the fear of loss of title or fortune. These are obnoxious to the populace, and are daily becoming more so; they commit grave errors; they promote disorder in all the administrations; before long they will be overturned by the people, and in any event their opinions will alienate the healthy elements of the population.

The party of the Republic is composed of the middle class, the youthful generation, and the people. I cannot attach myself to the former, and, moreover, even if I did it would profit nothing to the party itself, since before a fortnight is over it will suffice for these gentlemen to make a proposition to have it rejected by the people. *My sympathies, on the other hand, are not with the Republic, but with the individuals who compose the Republican party.* (Italics do not exist in the text.—H. R. W.) One thing I can do, and will readily undertake, should your Majesty aid me in its execution. I would endeavour to form from out of the middle class itself *a party for the union of Lombardy with Piedmont*, nor do I despair of accomplishing it.

But such a party will not be inspired with aristocratic aims, and I will not seek to form it unless I can vouchsafe your Majesty's acceptance of the demands it may formulate. It would assuredly not consent to unite itself with Piedmont such as is Piedmont today, accepting existing institutions, laws, &c. But it might agree to place itself under the same *régime* should institutions adapted to its needs be granted Lombardy. If it be accorded me to form this party, your Majesty may rely on having real partisans in Lombardy among enlightened, distinguished, and influential persons.

But, for the love of the salvation of Italy, let not your Majesty delude yourself on the possession of a real party whilst only the nobles and officials of Milan are with you. These will soon fall, while even should they continue to exist they will have no influence with the population. I have given no definite reply to the representative of the foreign power who approached me, because, before accepting such a mission as the leadership of a party, I desire to assure myself that such a party could exist and wield some power—facts which must depend on the care your Majesty gives to the formation of a party from among the middle classes.

May your Majesty deign to forgive this frank statement, and consider only the sentiment which dictates my words. I await the reply it may please your Majesty to have transmitted to me, and I lay at your feet the homage of my respectful devotion.—Brofferio, *Storia del Parlamento Subalpino;* also Costa de Beauregard, *Charles Albert,* vol. ii.

One is tempted to smile at the calm assumption with which the writer implies that she holds the key of the solution of a grave political crisis in the hollow of her hand. Yet, sceptical as we are inclined to be concerning the hypothetical representative of a "friendly foreign power" so confidingly disposed to entrust the impulsive princess with the direction of a party destined to balance, or hold in check, the extremists whose contentions threaten the efficacy of Charles Albert's intervention, we must, nevertheless, admit certain claims to the pretensions she advanced, farfetched though they undoubtedly were.

Although Charles Albert took no official or direct notice of the princess's communication, messages were conveyed to her through intermediaries, proving that her suggestions were not regarded in the light of an impertinence.

Writing under date of April 21st, Count Castagneto forwarded a copy of the princess's letter to the Chevalier Farina in strict confidence, he urges:

Do not speak of it to a soul in the world, such being the desire of His Majesty, but use it for your own information, and then write me. Manage also to see the princess herself, and without showing that you know anything, tell her that you are charged by me to salute her, and to inform her that in connection with the affair of which she wrote it would be necessary to know the conditions, but that she is relied upon to a much greater extent than any other person.—Brofferio, *op. cit.*

That further communications passed between the princess and Charles Albert, or his representatives, seems probable, since Castagneto, on June 15th, transmits to the same correspondent the following instructions:

. . . If you see the Belgiojoso, give her my compliments, and impress upon her that a simple declaration of fusion, with a mixed ministry which shall immediately assume the direction of affairs, is the only possible salvation.—Brofferio, *op. cit.*

Charles Albert realised the advisability of placating the Republican and Democratic factions in Milan. To Mazzini he sent offering to confer personally with him, provided certain conditions were accepted. In her comprehensive biography of the great agitator, Madame Venturi asserts that the king actually offered Mazzini the premiership of a government constructed on Democratic lines: documentary evidence of this astounding proposition would seem, however, to be lacking.

Among the conditions stipulated for by the princess, in view of the formation and direction by her of a political party pledged to support Charles Albert and unity with Piedmont, was the transfer of the national capital from Turin to Milan. As in the old days, it was urged that Turin was strategically ill-suited for a seat of government, while both geographically and politically Milan met the requirements of an Italian Kingdom which was to stretch from the ports of the Mediterranean to those of the Adriatic. That this difficulty would have been satisfactorily disposed of had Charles Albert been successful in his military campaign and in joining hands with Venice there is some reason to believe.

With many another, however, Donna Christina began to realise that for the present local ambitions must give place to the weightier demands of political fusion. To wrangle over forms while Radetzky was still master of the Quadrilateral meant to compromise the advantages gained at such heroic sacrifice.

The princess, with characteristic determination, now threw herself unreservedly into the Fusionist movement. Her facile pen and eloquent persuasiveness were devoted without stint or measure to the furtherance of the patriotic cause. Establishing herself in Milan, her days were given up to the editing and composition of her journals and pamphlets and the winning of converts from among the frequenters of her hastily organised *salon*.

The chaos which surrounded the Provisional Government, and for which she held its members individually responsible, provoked her bitterest comment. *"L'Insurrection Lombarde et le Gouvernement provisoire de Milan,"* published in the *Revue des Deux Mondes* of September 15, 1848, teems with often unsubstantiated accusation and peevish criticism. Count Casati, his colleague Borromeo, and other prominent members of the Provisional Government, meet with but scant justice at her hands: their personal motives are impugned; their administrative acts subjected to captious censure. The reader becomes painfully conscious of the note of personal spite underlying the professedly impartial and at times really masterly narration of the entanglements of a Municipal Council suddenly invested with the complex attributes of a Provisional Government which included among its dignitaries a Minister of War. Contemporary criticism is more lenient in its appreciation of Count Casati:

> . . . This man, who, in spite of his official position, necessitating continuous intercourse with the Government authorities, impersonated during the months which preceded the revolution the native antagonism to the foreigner. His speech, never provocative, yet vibrated with offended dignity, and resounded with an accent of protest which neither threats nor flattery could silence. Milan, in her struggle with the Austrian Government, felt herself faithfully represented by Mayor Casati.—Address by Gaetano Negri before Patriotic Associations of Milan, June 9, 1885.

A couple of years earlier (1846) the princess had published, in Paris, a pamphlet wherein she lashed unmercifully the political apathy of her fellow-citizens. That she libelled the physical courage of her compatriots in her *Etudes sur l'histoire de la Lombardie dans les trente dernièr es années, ou des causes du défaut d'énergie chez les Lombards,* (Studies on the history of Lombardy in the last thirty years, or causes of the lack of energy in the Lombards), the glorious "Five Days" attest. Again, even the paltry internecine dissensions of the victorious insurrectionists; their uncertainties and fatal hesitations; their lack of political solidarity or discipline—in a word, the absence of any representative appreciation of the moral responsibilities created by their material success—would hardly justify the harsh estimate formed by the princess in that pessimistic essay.

CHAPTER 8

Rumours of Treachery

Not content with her epistolary intercourse with Charles Albert, Donna Christina sought a personal interview. The king, however, for reasons of which we are unaware, deputed Count Castagneto to receive the princess. Into his ears she was consequently fain to pour her entreaties that the monarch whom the Turinese wags had dubbed "*Re Tentennio*" ("King Wobble") would show himself firm and resolute in a crisis which called for the iron hand of a Bismarck or the diplomacy of a Cavour.

It was at Lodi, within a few miles of the Lombard capital, that on August 2, 1848, the Princess Belgiojoso sought an interview with the king. We can imagine the passionate note in her pleading with Count Castagneto. Rumours of treachery followed as each fresh check or defeat of the Piedmontese arms leaked out. In Milan the Republicans, Mazzini at their head, were losing patience: already signs of the abandonment of their neutrality were evident. The Provincial Government had fallen into discredit: suspicion and distrust pervaded the city, and the Milanese press was decidedly menacing in tone.

Although the princess was still personally loyal, she realised that unless some signal and resolute action was taken the wavering allegiance of the half-won Mazzinians would be irrevocably forfeited. Alone they could accomplish little, it was true, but their open defection must dangerously complicate an already perilous situation. Should the support of Charles Albert be withdrawn, broken reed though it had proved, it became apparent to the veriest tyro that the sublime heroism of the Five Days had been a useless holocaust.

Blunder after blunder, political and military, had now irrevocably compromised the brilliant prospects under which the Piedmontese forces had taken the field. Himself but an indifferent military commander, Charles Albert lacked moral courage to resign into more

STREET FIGHTING IN MILAN

competent hands the personal direction of strategical operations. Reliance on the inspirations of mysticism, combined with a religious bigotry which insisted on making military operations subservient to the celebration of masses, had dissipated the splendid opportunities presented at the outset of the campaign, while Radetzky was dragging his demoralised and dispirited column—stretching over fifteen miles in straggling disorder—to the cover of the fortresses of the Quadrilateral. Costa de Beauregard wrote:—

The king kills himself with maceration and prayer.

And with ever greater frequency he sought strategical inspiration from the ecstatic communications which an hysterical Savoyard nun, Sister Marie Thérèse, transmitted from the asylum where she was confined. (*Les Dernières années du Roi Charles Albert.*)

The defection of the Pope and King of Naples from the Nationalist cause, while reducing numerically the forces on which he could rely, strengthened Charles Albert's personal prestige, leaving to him alone among Italian princes the patriotic task of ousting the foreigner. Superior in number to the forces at Radetzky's disposal, the Italian host was, moreover, inspired with an enthusiasm which guaranteed a moral supremacy when confronted by the dejected forces rallying round the forlorn hope which the genius of Radetzky alone preserved from rout.

The Austrian commander took immediate advantage of each successive blunder made by his incapable and hesitating opponent, whose attention, divided as it was between religious observances and scruples concerning the political and diplomatic aspects of his position, was constantly diverted from the strategical obligations of the military situation. Reinforcements reached the Austrians, who step by step recovered the lost ground, while Charles Albert as gradually fell back.

Already Radetzky was marching on Milan. On August 2nd, the day of the princess's attempt to see the king, the Austrians attacked the bridge of Lodi, which the retreating Piedmontese hastily destroyed. Charles Albert now sought shelter under the walls of Milan.

The city was again bristling with barricades thrown up by the panic-stricken inhabitants, who determined to fall fighting rather than risk the fierce reprisals of Radetzky's infuriated Croats and Slavs.

Men, women, and children held themselves prepared to sell dearly the lives they offered to their country.—*Princess Belgiojoso in Revue des Deux Mondes.*

A committee of Public Safety, hastily constituted at the prompting of Mazzini, made plans for a second siege, victualled the town, organised defences, and decreed the levy of the National Guard. The arrival of Charles Albert brought a short-lived relief, which the king's refusal to enter the city, together with the inexplicable disposal of the forces still available, rapidly converted into sullen suspicion, followed later by frenzy on the part of the mob. The people anxiously awaited an official declaration from the king concerning his plans for their defence.

None such being forthcoming, the Princess Belgiojoso, convinced that the people only needed a signal to co-operate with the military, betook herself to the Committee of Public Safety, and urged that a proclamation be issued making clear the resolutions adopted by the king and government for the protection of the city.

> I had the promise that my advice would be followed. While I was still with the Committee, other persons arrived making the same demand.—*Op. cit.*

Notwithstanding these assurances, fearing a possible misunderstanding between the king and people concerning the defence of the city, the princess hurried to the squalid little inn outside the walls where Charles Albert was provisionally lodged, and made known her errand to Count Castagneto. The king's secretary listened attentively, and reassured his interlocutor with the assertion that his royal master would defend Milan at all costs: of this there could be no possible question, since Charles Albert had preferred falling back on the city to re-crossing the Ticino into Piedmont. The princess adds:

> I retired, begging him to congratulate the king on the resolution he had taken, and after impressing on him that the public peace depended on its execution.

In her interesting account of subsequent events, of which she was an eye-witness, the princess states that Milan could count for its defence on some fifty thousand National Guards and thirtythree pieces of artillery, exclusive of the twenty-five thousand Piedmontese regulars. Moreover, the populace was ready and eager to renew the struggle of the preceding March, shoulder to shoulder with the military. The anomaly of the situation lay in the hesitation of the chief, to whom all eyes were turned, to assume the direction of affairs and resolutely place himself at the head of the expectant patriots.

We now know that in coming to fight under the walls of Milan, Charles Albert obeyed a chivalrous instinct—an action which the peculiar nature of the man can alone explain. In itself a strategical error, and clearly recognised as such, it was undertaken in the hope that a more advantageous capitulation might be secured, and the sack of the city, together with the excesses attendant thereon, be avoided. (Talleyrand-Périgord, *Guerre de Lombardie*.)

On the 4th of August, the Austrians attacked the Piedmontese troops, the fighting being fiercest along the lines outside the Porta Romana. The personal bravery displayed by Charles Albert amounted, as usual, to temerity. The king seemed to court death, and looked with envy on those who fell at his side.

The princess relates that she saw the workers on the barricades forced to suspend their labours owing to the rain of shells falling among them. On this occasion, the conduct under fire of the untried National Guard would seem to have been exemplary. The impetuosity of the defence of their positions resulted in the repulse of the aggressors. Popular enthusiasm over this initial success leaped at a bound from exaltation to fanaticism. With the return of self-confidence, the ineradicable distrust of Charles Albert revived. The king, no longer in safety, sought refuge within the city walls. Making his way to the Palazzo Greppi through streets furrowed with trenches and heaped with the incongruous miscellany of the hastily constructed barricades, the unhappy king "drained of mental and moral strength," could not fail to note the marks of popular scorn or humiliating indifference his passage excited.

Charles Albert had expressed his determination not to enter Milan until the Austrians had been driven back. This sudden and inexplicable change of plans engendered feelings of uneasiness which even the enthusiasm aroused by the creditable performance of the National Guard were powerless to dispel. Rumours of a secret capitulation began to be whispered among a population whose martial ardour, far from being daunted, was impatient for the fray. The very mention of such an inconceivable calamity so infuriated the mob that two misguided patriots who publicly announced the possible capitulation were literally torn to pieces, under the impression that they were Austrian sympathisers seeking to create discord between the military and the populace.

But the rumour spread with lightning rapidity. A lively recollection of the humiliating discomfiture inflicted on Radetzky's half-savage Croatians a few months earlier, fired the popular imagination as to the nature of probable reprisals. The princess exclaims:

A fate all the more horrible because inevitable was felt to be in store for Milan.

It was affirmed that the Piedmontese were about to retire; that the military and civil authorities were either already in flight or preparing to follow the king; that the population thus shamefully abandoned was to be delivered over to Radetzky and his bloodthirsty hordes:

I cannot attempt to describe the consternation of a people from whom victory was thus snatched before the struggle. We were all mad with grief: hiding their faces in their hands the men wept; the women, more used to tears, more frightened and less ashamed of lamentation, ran frantically from street to street uttering shrieks of terror. I myself saw an old man fall dead on the announcement of the dread news, and the earth ran red with his blood. My ears were lacerated by the unaccustomed din; I now beheld a spectacle such as even the delirium of fever never conjured from my diseased imagination.

Finally rage succeeds despair. The irritated mob, determined to prevent the flight of the king, and to force him to repudiate the infamous capitulation, marches on the Greppi Palace. A squad of mounted police on guard receives orders to retire on the approach of the mob in order not to further incite popular exasperation. In an instant, the royal carriages are overturned; barricades constructed; the Palace surrounded and invaded; a deputation of the National Guard questions Charles Albert concerning the capitulation.

He denies it; then he is forced against his will to follow the deputation on the balcony, whence he harangues the people, apologises for his ignorance of the real feelings of the Milanese, declares himself well pleased to find them so eager for the struggle, and solemnly promises to fight at their head to the last drop of his blood, A shot or two is fired at Charles Albert. With the last words of his harangue the indignant populace cries, 'If it is so, destroy the capitulation.' The king then draws a piece of paper from his pocket, he holds it aloft so that the people see it; then he tears it to shreds.

Another eye-witness, the eminent Milanese historian Cantu, thus describes the thrilling scene on the balcony:

I was at his side when he began to speak. But his voice was too weak to make itself heard. I asked him what he desired to say, offering myself as a mouthpiece. He pronounced some sentences which the howling of the crowd prevented my catching. At this moment, a bullet whistled between us. The king made a gesture of compassion with his hand, pointed to the infuriated mob, and withdrew.

Either from the balcony or to the delegation within the palace, the king undoubtedly gave his word that the defence of Milan, and the war, should be continued in deference to popular opinion. Under this impression the mob dispersed, and the gates of the palace were closed. Yet it required but the accidental explosion of a neighbouring powder-magazine to arouse afresh frenzied suspicions of treachery. Again, the palace is besieged by the maddened populace, led, it is claimed, by the dregs of the prisons of Mantua, liberated by Radetzky in order to foment disturbances and incite revolt. "Citizen Charles Albert" is summoned to deliver himself over to the people. Others claim his son, the Duke of Genoa, as a hostage until the king's pledges are fulfilled. Others, again, insist on a written declaration signed by the royal hand.

With a sigh Charles Albert obeys:

What matters it that I die today or tomorrow!

In a trice, the walls of Milan are covered with the royal proclamation:

The energetic manner in which the people have pronounced against any negotiations with the enemy determines me to continue the struggle in spite of adverse conditions. I remain with you as amidst my children. . . ."

Again, panic seized upon the unreasoning mob, which professed to recognise in the burning for strategical purposes of some woods and hovels beside the walls, a fiendish project of Charles Albert's to reduce their city to ashes. The square before the palace is invaded for the third time; but now it is the king's life the mob demands. A rain of bullets is directed against the windows, and an attempt made to burn or destroy the portals.

Cut off from any communication with his troops, Charles Albert's plight was extremely critical until Colonel La Marmora, escaping in the darkness over a wall giving on a narrow side street, hastened, at the peril of his life, to summon a Piedmontese regiment.

At midnight the king, escorted by his faithful *bersaglieri*, left the palace on foot, and abandoned the city by the Porta Vercellina, in strict accordance with the stipulations of his secret contract with Radetzky; and with him the Piedmontese Army silently stole away.

When the retreat of the Piedmontese became known, consternation and confusion reigned supreme. The vilest epithets, the bitterest curses, were freely lavished by the populace upon the head of the unhappy sovereign. The Milanese found themselves without a leader and bereft of the moral support of even the Committee of Public Safety, whose members, headed by Mazzini, took refuge at Lugano, there to reorganise, and later become identified with the insurrectionist *Junta*.

The Austrians announced a truce of twelve hours before they entered the city, and accorded liberty of action to all such as might prefer exile to submission to the old *régime*.

The princess says:

> This alternative was availed of with joy by the miserable people. More than two-thirds of the population—men, women, the aged and the young, rich and poor—sought escape by the gate furthest removed from the one by which the Austrians were to enter. An interminable column of emigrants of every age, sex, and condition! All carried with them their most precious possessions; those they held most dear, their children, the sick whom they dared not leave to the fury of the Croats or the discretion of the victor.

In his account of the scene, of which he was also an eye-witness, Comte de Reiset, the French Envoy in Milan, says that Charles Albert's departure was followed by *"une émigration effrayante"*—"A scary emigration." (*Mes Souvenirs*, vol. i.) This is somewhat vague; but the princess's estimate that the exodus included "nearly one hundred thousand Milanese" would appear excessive.

Be this as it may, however, Piedmont and the neighbouring cantons of the Swiss Confederation afforded temporary shelter to vast numbers of Lombards of all social grades, who dared not face the consequences of their patriotic fervour during the "Five Days," or their rebellious action in participating in the late campaign. Notwithstanding Radetzky's promises, the troops wreaked a savage vengeance on their cowed and defenceless foe. The palaces of the Lombard aristocrats who had taken a conspicuous part in the revolution were sacked, notably the homes of the Litta, Borromeo, and Belgiojoso.

CHAPTER 9

Princess Seeks Support of France

Humiliated, discouraged, but untamed, the Princess Belgiojoso, in company with thousands of her compatriots, again trod the road to exile. The home in Paris was still in her possession, and France attracted her the more since the insipid July Monarchy had given place to the Republic which was to elect Prince Napoleon as its head.

Yet in spite of the bitterness of her deception, Donna Christina refuses to pass judgment on Charles Albert, whose motives she frankly confesses incomprehensible. Her article in the *Revue des Deux Mondes*, (October 1, 1848), written barely six weeks after the tragic events she describes, is a vindication of her fellow-citizens, not an indictment of treachery against the unhappy king. Its conclusions display a moderation which cannot fail to surprise those who have in mind the impetuosity with which the princess is wont to throw herself into the political *mêlée*. She tells what she believes to be the truth, and tells it fearlessly, but is nevertheless willing to admit that the other side may hold in reserve arguments worthy of patriotic consideration.

She wrote:

Concerning the accusations against Charles Albert, if the facts we have exposed clearly substantiate them, yet, on the other hand, the arguments in his favour advanced by his friends are not without interest. To those who affirm that the conduct of Charles Albert was the natural consequence of the mistrust inspired by the democratic tendencies of the Lombards, to those who do not hesitate to proclaim it treason, the upholders of Charles Albert offer elucidations of some value. Whatever the fear of Charles Albert concerning the democratic tendencies of Lombardy, does it seem more probable that he would have betrayed the Milanese rather than break up and destroy the plots which so greatly disquieted him? Is it not necessary to have courage to enact a treachery? And the dangers to which a traitor exposes himself, are they not most serious?

If the King of Piedmont did not dismiss his generals, if he did not adopt more energetic and bolder measures, the explanation must be sought in his irresolute and weak character. If he signed the capitulation, the blame must rest on those who painted the people in such dark colours that he had no confidence in the energy of the citizens. He feared for the city the rage of a ferocious victor, of an unbridled soldiery: he dreaded the license of the Croats, unleashed in a city taken by assault.

The princess is willing to concede that national and international political antipathies of a more personal nature might also have their weight, but she wisely contends that the time for raising the veil is not yet. The last act of the drama is still pending. None as yet, excepting perhaps the wretched king himself, could foresee the *dénouement* of the tragedy, the scene of which was to be laid under the walls of Novara five months later, when defeat, abdication, flight, exile, and death closed the career of him whom Mazzini had styled the "Hamlet of Italian Independence."

Donna Christina urges:

In the meantime, Italians still stand facing their common foe; let the question of responsibilities be postponed; let all party strife, hatred, and jealousy be made subservient to the great issue of Nationality.

Let us trust, then, that the honour of Italy will be vindicated: discord must not weaken such generous impulse: our independence once achieved will be recognised for ever.—*Revue des Deux Mondes*, October 1, 1848.

The princess acknowledged no insurmountable obstacle, physical or moral. The scandal of schism might tarnish the political ideal; accusations of sloth or treachery be preferred against individuals; but she was one of those upon whom the shattering of long-cherished hopes and patient endeavour has a stimulating effect, leaving them undismayed and prepared to resume their task with redoubled energy and with confidence unimpaired. Conspiracy had filled the cravings for romantic action in her youth: now, in her maturity, she felt the need of strenuous effort in the open.

The fierce light of battle had beaten round her; she had witnessed the collective and individual abnegation of the fellow-citizens, as well as their petty foibles and conceits, and unhesitatingly, without idealising the one or minimising the other, she accepted the former as outweighing the latter. Nor was her loyalty to and belief in the House of Savoy vitally weakened. Politically, Charles Albert was still a possibility to be reckoned with, although after the capitulation of Milan it was with a chastened enthusiasm that she championed her knight.

Unlike the traditional *femme politique*, however, the Princess Belgiojoso in reality looked for national regeneration and independence through the popular acceptance of an abstract principle rather than by the imposition of any concrete formula or personality. And therein lay at once the strength and the weakness of her political philosophy. A leader there must be; but whether the indispensable directing energy were furnished by prince or people was immaterial. Mazzini or Charles Albert—Republic or Monarchy—what mattered the form, the figure-head, provided the essential principles underlying Liberty and Independence be attained and preserved?

Animated by sentiments such as these, the princess on her return to Paris resumed with tireless energy the patriotic propaganda which sought to revive French sympathy with the plight of Italy.

The diplomats had for some time past been occupied with the vexed question of an Austrian preponderance which, it was beginning to be realised abroad, constituted an ever-increasing source of discontent and revolt in the Peninsula.

During the early stages of the war with Austria the Piedmontese Government had shown itself decidedly opposed to intervention by France. The Marquis Pareto in conversation with Sir Ralph Abercromby, the British Minister at Turin, urged:

We hold to it absolutely, that it be known that Italy *farà da se* (will act unaided).

And he added that he had gone so far as to request the French Government to withdraw the army of the Alps from close proximity to the frontier, lest its presence give rise to a misconstruction of Italian aims and ambitions. (De Reiset, *op. cit.* vol. i.) During the high tide of military success, it was deemed—and correctly so—that foreign intervention must entail a diminution of national prestige, whereby Piedmont would infallibly forfeit a measure of popular confidence throughout the Peninsula. In May, the Austrian Minister in London

NAPOLEON III.

had signified the willingness of his government to cede Lombardy, under certain conditions; but Charles Albert echoed the national sentiment when he demanded the total and unconditional expulsion of the foreigner and the untrammelled liberty of the populations to select their own form of government.

But the confidence of Italians in their ability to work out unaided their own salvation was not after all sufficiently deep-rooted to withstand the moral shock, disaster following so closely on the military successes inaugurated with the Milanese revolt. Although popular sentiment opposed foreign mediation, official prudence recognised, after the turn of the tide of military prosperity, the utility of an understanding with Paris and London. In response to tentative proceedings, France and England tendered their good offices towards a settlement of issues presenting such grave difficulties to both sides that Austria, notwithstanding her apparent advantages, deemed it advisable to accede to the proffered mediation.

Charles Albert was destined, however, to derive no benefit from this appeal to diplomacy. Events at home soon made it manifest that he must choose between civil war or a renewal of a struggle which presented from the outset odds foreshadowing defeat. Novara (March 23, 1849) not only humbled Piedmont in the dust, but crushed the spirit of the Nationalist movement, retarding by a decade Italian political regeneration.

The Paris to which Christina Belgiojoso returned after her flight from Milan offered the anomalous spectacle of a Republic preparing to elect as its chief an Imperial prince whose personal ambitions were even then an open secret. The sham democracy and hypocritical proletarian enthusiasms of the "*Bourgeois* King" had proved his undoing; yet France, with open eyes, was again courting the destruction of the principles of popular government for the integral maintenance of which the revolution of February had been undertaken. Society, or such portions of it as pretended to political influence, was tentatively feeling its way, probing the shifting sands of democracy for the foundations whereupon to build the Imperialism which was to last a generation.

In the official world of this period of transition the figure of the Princess Belgiojoso was a familiar one. The Vicomte de Beaumont-Vassy, (*Les Salons de Paris*), gives some curious details of a great ball she attended, during the month of August, at the residence of Monsieur Marrast, president of the *Assemblée Constituante*. The princess had attired herself for this occasion in a costume supposed to represent Italy. Dressed in a startling robe composed of the national colours (red, white, and green), she was a conspicuous figure in the motley cosmopolitan assemblage of diplomatists, government officials, and worldlings whose curiosity had impelled attendance. Of a sudden the ballroom was invaded by a jostling crowd of National Guards, blacksmiths, shoemakers, masons, house-painters, and that peculiarly Parisian product, the dog's barber, all political friends of "Citizen" Marrast, and as such convinced that a warm welcome awaited them.

Alas for the frailty of political asseverations! The dogma of social equality proclaimed so loudly on the Place de la Concorde, in the face of a mob intoxicated with the enthusiasm of success, became an embarrassing tenet in the presence of this glittering gathering of an international official and hereditary aristocracy. To their chagrin, the unwelcome intruders were somewhat unceremoniously ejected, protesting the while against a treatment so little in accord with the principles advanced by their political idol, whose personal influence had proved so powerful a lever in overturning the late *régime* of egotism and hypocrisy.

Yet although the princess did not allow herself to become a prey to painful retrospection, the winter of 1848-49 was fraught with keen anxiety for one who held the destiny of Italy as close to heart as she. Ever mindful of the social side of her propaganda, she again threw open the doors of her salon, welcoming with special graciousness those whose personal relations with Prince Napoleon promised political influence.

The armed peace in Piedmont, as costly as war, was rapidly draining Charles Albert's none too plethoric Exchequer; while the prolongation of the armistice not only humiliated the country, but strained to the point of revolt the patience of the ill-fed and poorly lodged troops. Moderates and Democrats wrangled noisily, mutually impugning each other's motives, complicating and entangling national issues, and postponing achievement by an academic war of words as egotistical as futile.

Interest centred, however, in Rome, where Count Rossi, appointed Prime Minister by Pius IX. in September, was in the following November assassinated by his political enemies. Although the Pope had never explicitly declared war on Austria, his troops had marched forth to the support of Charles Albert. The Pontiff was popularly believed to share the growing enthusiasm for national independence. He had, moreover, given an earnest of his sympathy with the reform movement by the grant of Constitutional liberties within the States of the Church. A composite Ministry, including ecclesiastics and laymen of repute and influence, had been formed with Mamiani, a fellow-exile and intimate of the Princess Belgiojoso, at its head. Mamiani was a Democrat in the most primitive and literal sense of the word, and a social reformer to boot.

It soon became apparent that popular Constitutional Government and Theocracy were incompatible on the lines he followed, and he was succeeded by Rossi, who had been French Ambassador at the Papal Court. Rossi, somewhat of a doctrinaire, and a diplomatist rather than a statesman, combined with frank and determined objection to Democracy strong leanings towards Nationalism, and decided, if less open, sympathies with Liberalism. But the policy he adopted was uncongenial to the people and rendered him hateful to the Democrats, while to the Jesuits, whose suppression in France he had formerly been commissioned to negotiate, he was particularly obnoxious. The knife of an unknown assassin struck him dead as he went to open what promised to be an epoch-making session of the Chamber. Democrat or Jesuit? Each placed the odium of the deed at the other's door.

The result, however, left the Democrats practical masters of the situation. A menacing crowd demanded of the Pope an immediate acceptance of the Democratic programme and pledges for its fulfilment. The Pope refused "to treat with rebels," and the Swiss Guard imprudently attempted to overawe the demonstration by the discharge of their firearms. The native troops, on the other hand, sided with the people and attacked the Quirinal Palace where the Pope was in residence. Yielding to force, Pius, protesting, acceded to the popular clamour, and peace was restored. But the Pope was thoroughly alarmed, and during the night of November 25th, disguised as a common priest, accompanied by the wife of the Bavarian Minister, he fled Rome, taking refuge at Gaeta, in the dominions of Ferdinand of Naples.

The flight of the Pope and the resignation of those constituted in authority by him, left Rome at the mercy of the populace. It was not until the following February that the Assembly met. In the meanwhile, the world beheld the amazing spectacle of an excited and hot-headed populace held in check by the moderation and sound common sense of an ignorant wine-carrier of the Trastevere.

The news of the Pope's flight reached Paris on November 28,

1848. The true significance of the events which had prompted the Pontiff to abandon his States, was imperfectly appreciated when General Cavaignac suggested that France send troops to Civita Vecchia for the protection of the Pope. Anarchy was said to rule in Rome, and the patriots who had the best interests of their country at heart recognised that the spread of popular license could only be detrimental to their cause. As a consequence, the Princess Belgiojoso and her friends were inclined to view with equanimity, if not positive satisfaction, an intervention which promised to offset Austrian preponderance in the vexed Italian problem.

Since her interview in London, Christina Belgiojoso had cherished the belief that Louis Bonaparte would one day redeem his pledges in Italy. The Napoleonic triumph of December 10, 1848, "crowning the Republic with a name which is, one might say, its negation," (C. de Mazade, *Monsieur Thiers*), filled her with jubilation. That the Prince-President presaged the emperor affected her enthusiasm not a whit. Her Republicanism was, as we have seen, intermittent, resting on no sound foundation of personal conviction or belief in its efficacy as a panacea for her country's ills. Despite his personal shortcomings and his misfortunes (perhaps because of the latter, since she was a woman) the Belgiojoso's sympathies with Charles Albert remained unimpaired, even after Novara had sealed his doom.

But like many of her compatriots she turned to France for that substantial protection against Austria which Charles Albert had proved himself powerless to guarantee. Of the disinterestedness of the French intervention she would seem at this period to have entertained no suspicion; or at least to have gone no further than the assumption that the destruction of Austrian supremacy in the Peninsula, with the attendant loss of European prestige, would prove a sufficient political compensation to France. Mazzini himself was deceived by the assurances he received from Ledru-Rollin, and other advanced Republicans, concerning the interpretation of the new French Constitution, which warranted the fullest sympathy and moral support to the politically oppressed. Again, the newly elected President had personally taken part in the struggle for reform in the Pope's dominions in 1831, and was, moreover, as a Carbonaro, pledged by solemn oath to aid in the liberation of Italy from the yoke of the hated foreigner.

French Catholics professed themselves outraged by the situation in Rome; and although the Pope himself mistrusted French intervention, and would have preferred to owe his reinstatement to Austria or

Spain, the opportunity presented tangible advantages which the none too stable situation in France made it imperative for the Government to seize. Of its morality, the less said the better, but subsequent events would seem to vouch for the expediency of the venture. A reactionary movement, which quickly swept the Republicans into a minority, followed the elections for the French Legislative Assembly, which succeeded the *Constituante*. Thiers, Odilon-Barrot, and Berryer, were prominent chiefs of this reactionary party, which, as the party of order, sought to purge the country of perilous revolutionary elements, to multiply social guarantees at home, and safeguard French prestige abroad. (De Mazade, *op cit.*) This was the party which sent a French army to Rome; such the beginnings of the reaction which three years later made the "Second of December" not only possible but inevitable.

Monsieur Thiers, as we know, at one time entertained an embarrassing sentimental admiration for the lovely Italian exile. But some sixteen years had passed; the princess was over forty years of age, and although her beauty and charm were still remarkable, time and circumstances had tempered the ardent passion of the little Marseillais. Between the two there existed, however, a very cordial friendship founded on mutual esteem and a community of intellectual interests and pursuits. Intimately associated also with the foremost political men of the day, and a close observer of the undercurrents of French politics—especially when Italy was concerned—we can but marvel that the princess was apparently so grossly deceived in regard to the meaning of the proposed intervention. Rather are we inclined to the belief that the situation in Rome, such as she knew it between November, 1848, and February, 1849, met with neither her sympathy nor approval.

Italian patriots were by no means in accord concerning the advantages to be obtained by the permanent dethronement of the Pope. Many looked upon the flight of Pius IX. and the abolition of his temporal power in Rome as a positive disaster for the National cause. We have grievously few and meagre records of the princess's personal sentiments during these months of uncertainty; but it is permissible to surmise that the news which reached her from Italy, as well as what she heard in France, painted the Roman crisis and all it must entail in unattractive colours.

Mazzini himself held back. On news of the Pope's flight he urgently appealed to his friends in Rome to agitate for a Republic. Yet his personal initiative, during the critical months when the wine-carrier

Ciceruacchio practically restrained the people's passions, was confined to correspondence. Contrary to what might have been expected, he appeared in no haste to take advantage of and personally develop the exceptional opportunity offered in Rome. Mazzini tarried in Tuscany until nearly a month after the decree proclaiming the Republic was issued, reaching Rome only on the evening of March 5th. Garibaldi with his nondescript followers trooped into the Eternal City about the same period.

One of the first acts of the Assembly had been the bestowal of citizenship on Mazzini, and the honour had been simultaneous with an invitation to Rome. On his arrival, the new Republic created him a Triumvir, along with Saffi and Armellini. Mazzini, however, soon eclipsed his colleagues, becoming dictator in all but name: a mild and lenient autocrat, but one whose authority was none the less real because benign.

Meanwhile, despite the establishment of the Roman Republic and Mazzini's plea for benevolent neutrality, France pushed forward preparations for the threatened intervention. The expedition, which it was officially affirmed came in order to protect the Romans against the evils of an Austrian occupation, arrived off Civita Vecchia on April 26, 1849. Landing unopposed, but in the face of the protest of the local authorities, General Oudinot marched his troops against a city before which he naively believed he had but to appear in order to take possession.

CHAPTER 10

The Princess is Dispossessed

When it became apparent that the French Republic contemplated strangling her tiny Roman sister in the cradle, the wrath of the Princess Belgiojoso knew no bounds. Perhaps her chagrin was embittered by the suspicion that she had been hoodwinked by her political friends in Paris. Perhaps the old glamour of Mazzini's idealism reasserted its sway, and, the irreparable disaster at Novara having absolved her of personal loyalty to Charles Albert's claims, she felt at liberty again to embrace Republicanism. Perhaps she was, after all, as much impelled by the old spirit of revolt and battle, the resistless craving for excitement and violent emotions, as by political considerations.

Whatever the impetus, her patriotism is unimpeachable. An opportunity offered to serve Italy, and she seized it unquestioningly. There never was even a bare fighting chance of success. Yet principles were involved which she had been among the first to recognise as vital, and by virtue of which alone Italians might dare hope for national autonomy. Whether the princess originally contemplated the hospital work to which she later devoted herself we cannot say; but there are indications which would seem to imply that circumstances imposed the task upon her.

Undismayed by the prospect of participating in a forlorn hope, the princess quitted Paris and journeyed in all haste to Rome.

Once more among her colleagues in conspiracy, the friends of exile, and the companions of the stirring days in Milan, the Belgiojoso is in her element. Surrounded by comrades such as Nino Bixio, Manara, the brothers Dandolo, her fellow-townsman Cernuschi—he who fought on the barricades at Milan in dancing-pumps and white tie, his perfumed locks flying in the breeze; by Bertani and Medici (later Garibaldi's most trusted lieutenants); by the patriot priest Ugo

Mrs. W. W. Story.

Bassi, the poet Mameli, and a host of minor lights, the princess again experiences the exhilaration of action. Of political propaganda, there is now no need. The Republic, that long-cherished, ever-illusive ideal of the brain of the man who now stands at its head, is for the nonce an established fact.

But our heroine had her hands full, nevertheless, for to her was confided the organisation and direction of the Roman hospitals. During the entire siege, together with an American, Margaret Fuller, and Julia Modena, *née* Calame, and connected with the great Swiss artist of that name, Donna Christina laboured incessantly for the relief and comfort of the wounded, the sick, and the dying. The role of *femme politique* is laid aside for that of a Sister of Charity. At the same time, the latter is supplemented by a very energetic and efficient hospital matron, who, when occasion demands, does not hesitate to beard the *Triumvirs* in their lair, exacting arrears of pay for her disabled military patients or redress for grievances connected with her administrative functions.

Among the foreigners who braved the siege, or a portion of it, were the well-known American sculptor, W. W. Story, and his wife. A note in the diary of the latter tells that on April 25th Margaret Fuller (or more correctly the Marchesa Ossoli, for she was secretly married to an Italian of that name) came to tell them:

> That all Rome was in a state of excitement, the news that the French had landed at Civita Vecchia having been received. We went with her to Piazza, del Popolo to hear the addresses made to the people, and there we met, standing on a bench, the Princess Belgiojoso.— Henry James, *W. W. Story*, vol. i.

A week later (May 2nd) the same hand records:

> We went with Margaret (Fuller) to the Pellegrini Hospital and gave our money, some 225 dollars, to Princess Belgiojoso. Then we went to Spillman's to get ice for the p
> rincess, and while there saw the burning of a cardinal's carriage, the blaze quite lighting up the front of the Propaganda.

Mr. Story also has his word to speak concerning our heroine. In his journal, under date of April 25 (1849), after describing the impression created in Rome by the news of the French landing, he continues:

> I met the Princess Belgiojoso, grown much older and negligently dressed. We walked along together up beyond the Pan-

theon, and I then left her. She was very cordial and agreeable, and pressed me to come and see her.—Henry James, *W. W. Story*, vol. i.

Amplifying his wife's record of the incident of May 2nd, the American sculptor writes:

... We went to carry our money to the Princess Belgiojoso, directress of all the hospitals, whom we found sitting surrounded with men and women, giving her various orders with calmness and clearness and showing the greatest practicality and good sense in all her arrangements. She has laid down strict rules and reduced the establishment to order and discipline; for three days and two nights she has been without sleep and still is strong. Then we went to Spillman's to get her an ice-cream to cool her parched throat.... Returning to the hospital, we carried our ice to the princess, and she partook of it, giving part to her little child, into whose stifling room I went to give it to her.

Again, on May 6th:

Went in the evening to the Trinità dei Pellegrini to carry the American subscription for the wounded in the late battle. Everything was in complete order—clean floors and beds, good ventilation, attendants gentle and without confusion. These the hospital owes to the princess, who has a genius for ordering and systematising. She said that nothing was more pleasant to her than to attend to the sick; it was, indeed, a sort of passion, for she added that in the sick-room one is *sure* of doing good. All efforts of charity in other directions may fail of their end—money given may be squandered or do injury, but the relief of physical pain is a thing definite and certain.—James, *op. cit.* vol. i.

When it became manifest that diplomacy had exhausted its cunning and that Oudinot was determined not only to occupy Rome but to reinstate the Pope and overthrow the Republic, the Assembly, led by Mazzini, and without a dissentient voice, decided on resistance at all costs. Barricades sprang up as if by magic and the people prepared for an energetic defence. On the morning of April 30th the French attack began. "Italians never fight!" sneered Oudinot; yet that day cost him nearly a thousand men. The raw Roman recruits fought like demons, driving their foe before them and forcing Oudinot to beat a hasty retreat to avoid being cut off from his base at Civita Vecchia.

Margaret Fuller wrote to Ralph Waldo Emerson:

It was a terrible battle, that of April 30th, fought here from dawn till the last light of day. I could see all its progress from my balcony. The Italians fought like lions. It is a truly heroic spirit that animates them. . . . Many, especially among the Lombards, are the flower of the Italian youth.

Realising his mistake in supposing the Romans disinclined to fight, Oudinot requested an armistice, which was immediately granted, and diplomatic negotiations were resumed.

Notwithstanding this initial success, the recognition that their Republic was doomed became apparent to government and citizens alike. Mazzini alone persisted in his belief that, in spite of Oudinot's aggression, relief would eventually come from France.

In the meanwhile, the Austrians, descending from the north, fell upon Bologna and Ancona, while Ferdinand of Naples advanced his troops over the frontier south of Rome, and Spain was preparing to land 5,000 men at Fumicino. Garibaldi made short work of "Bomba's" troops at Velletri (May 16th), and had the Romans been free to dispose of their forces even the Austrians might have been temporarily repulsed. But the combination—it was not technically a coalition—was too strong. The French general, his troops now numbering between thirty and forty thousand men, hurled himself (on June 2nd) against the sixteen thousand armed men, which was all the Romans could muster.

Although they lost their positions outside the walls, the Romans preserved the city and compelled Oudinot to begin operations for a regular siege. With a unanimity rare even in those days of patriotic fervour all classes accepted the bombardment, and the increasing suffering and want, without a murmur. Enthusiasm for the defence grew with its hopelessness.

Six thousand women offered their services for the hospitals, and as many as were needed did noble service under Princess Belgiojoso.—King, *Italian Unity*, vol. i.

The princess, although exercising a general supervision over all similar institutions, resided at and had under her special care the Pellegrini Hospital. To Margaret Fuller was entrusted that of the "*Fatebenefratelli.*" Mrs. Story wrote:

Night and day, Margaret was occupied, and, with the princess, so ordered and disposed the hospitals that the organisation was truly admirable. All the work was skilfully divided, so that there was no confusion or hurry, and from the chaotic condition in which these places had been left by those who had previously had charge of them they brought them to a state of perfect regularity and discipline.

The glowing tribute paid by her American friends is echoed by all those who came in contact with the princess during those eventful days.

Barbiera, (*Op. cit.*), draws a graphic picture of the Princess watching at the bedside of some restless patient and devouring the while by the feeble flicker of a taper the works of Charles Dickens, which were furnished her by Vieusseux from Florence. She writes to Vieusseux:

> When I begin to read anything of Dickens, I can't tear myself from it until I have read it ten times over.—Correspondence in National Library at Florence.

Alas! during those sad vigils interruptions must have been distractingly frequent.

Some of the notes she exchanged with the learned Genevan publisher and bookseller, whose library is still the rendezvous of the foreign colony in Florence, have been preserved. She writes at one time:

> Although most exhausted and also exposed to considerable danger, I feel, nevertheless, well and happy, because I am not called upon to witness an Italian disgrace. We may succumb, but we shall not, I hope, know dishonour. Greeting and brotherhood.

To which she adds in a postscript:

> I notice that I have ended in the Roman manner. It is the effect of habit.

The phraseology of classic Republicanism, greatly held to by Mazzini, had early been adopted in private as well as official correspondence, and was used even conversationally by purists. In her communications with the trio constituting the supreme authority the Princess addresses them as "Citizens *Triumvirs*," invariably terminating with the consecrated formula, "*Salute e fratellanza.*"

In another letter to Vieusseux she touches somewhat irritably on the political situation.

The stupidities of the *triumvirs* are many and various. The people are silent because a protest against the *triumvirs* might be interpreted as directed against the Republic. It is certain, however, that they are cooling, and that they do not actively exert themselves to support these men with whom they are not satisfied. In the face of the intervention the Roman people will, I fear, remain passive, not owing to indifference, as is said of some, but because of the small faith reposed in their leaders.—Correspondence in National Library at Florence.

Undoubtedly there had at first existed but slight enthusiasm for the Republic. By far the majority of the people felt it sufficient to have thrown off the intolerable rule of priests. They were willing enough to swear allegiance to any of the aristocracy who could show capability as a leader. "I respect the nobility, and never dream of being higher than they," had been Ciceruacchio's disclaimer when a vision of the heights to which he might climb had been disclosed to him. "I am a poor man of the people, and such I will always remain," was the remark by which he emphasised his modest protest. And Ciceruacchio probably expressed the sentiment of the class he represented.

The advent of Mazzini, his stirring eloquence, and the social reforms he promised, dazzled the patient Romans and gave a fillip to the somewhat academic, even anaemic, Republicanism which, *faute de mieux,* had been adopted. True, the equivocations during the months which elapsed between the Pope's flight and the proclamation of the Republic gave place, temporarily at least, to something like political assurance, but the Romans expected the impossible where their leaders were concerned, and the princess read correctly enough the signs of popular weakening not of physical courage, but of moral conviction. In a sense, perhaps, the Roman populace belied her estimate, for passive it certainly did not remain; yet, in spite of Mazzini's scathing denunciations, the Assembly preferred to adopt Garibaldi's more prudent counsel when advised of the futility of further sacrifice.

And there is reason for the suspicion that the threatening attitude of the populace, after a sullen surrender, was the outcome rather of wounded pride and a lively dread of consequences than of despair at the destruction of a political ideal. Again, the friction existing between Mazzini and Garibaldi, with the inevitably resultant intrigues and insidious criticism, was no mean factor in the development and spread of popular mistrust.

DANIELE MANIN

Among her patients at the hospital Donna Christina received that dashing young soldier, Nino Bixio, and the war-poet, Goffredo Mameli whose stirring verses beginning:

Fratelli d'Italia,
L'Italia s'è desta
(Brothers of Italy,
Italy has fallen)

. . . .fired the martial spirit of his countrymen throughout the length and breadth of Italy. To her it was given to soothe and comfort in his last agony one whose genius and life were cheerfully laid on the altar of Patriotism, and to close the eyes of the poet whose immortal verses will be remembered as long as the story of Italy's heroic struggle for Independence. Bixio's wounds were less serious, and, thanks to the princess's devoted care, he lived to achieve fame under Garibaldi's leadership during the epic conquest of Sicily and overthrow of the Bourbon *régime* at Naples.

Donna Christina was, however, not much longer to be allowed to carry on her noble work. On July 1st the Assembly decreed, "In the name of God and the People," the cessation of a defence which it was universally acknowledged had become impossible. Like the Roman senators of old, the members of the Assembly remained in their seats; and when three days later the French took possession of the city they found the legislators deliberating the new Constitution, which, notwithstanding the irony of the proceeding, was voted in due form. (Tivaroni, *L'Italia duranti il Dominio Austriaco*, vol. ii.)

Princess Belgiojoso and her devoted assistants were unceremoniously dispossessed by the French officials, who, not content with banishing the Italian surgeons and prohibiting the employment of female attendants, ordered the transfer of all patients, "except those to whom Extreme Unction had been administered," to the Termini prison. An attempt was made to justify this inexplicable proceeding on the plea of economy.

In a scathing letter, published in the Concordia at Turin, the princess denounces the new regime in unmeasured terms. According to her statement the Italian surgeons, of whom one was Bertani, of Garibaldian fame, gave their services gratuitously, and consequently no economy was effected by their "brutal discharge." The indictment, while dealing chiefly with technical details of administration, contains specific accusations of grave spiritual coercion exercised over the unfortunate patients. She wrote:

> You have permitted the dismissal of the chaplains, and have replaced them by fanatical Capuchin monks, who threaten to leave the wounded to perish of hunger and thirst unless they incontinently confess, and unless their confession betake of a political rather than a religious nature.—*La Concordia*, Turin, September 21, 1849.

The responsibility for such allegations must rest with the princess. It has been impossible to substantiate them in any contemporaneous records at our disposal, nor does Doctor Bertani's journal make any reference thereto. (J. W. Mario, *Agostino Bertani*.) Mazzini's parting injunctions exhorted, it is true, the Romans to perpetual protest, and urged them "to maintain the character of conquest throughout the occupation and to isolate the enemy." (Tivaroni, *op. cit*) . That the princess obeyed literally the injunctions of the uncompromising Triumvir, we have no difficulty in believing; but we cannot admit that she would deliberately issue statements for which no foundation existed.

Notwithstanding her bitter resentment of what she considered an unwarrantable interference with her work, Donna Christina remained in Rome all through July. Her present preoccupations were not, however, exclusively concerned with the relief of the suffering inmates of the hospitals and the amelioration of their sanitary and spiritual surroundings. The uncertainty of her own immediate future demanded anxious consideration.

With the temporary exception of Venice, every State and province of Italy had fallen once more under the yoke of the oppressor—foreign or domestic. Piedmont alone preserved a Constitutional form of Government.

Over the city of the lagoons Daniel Manin still upheld the banner of the Republic. Authoritative, ill-brooking contradiction or restraint, the Venetian patriot was withal no despot. Nor were his ambitions autocratic, as his enemies sought to represent, he exclaimed: "Doge of Venice? my ambitions soared far higher: I hardly dare confess it: Washington!"—Manin, *Pensieri staccato*, cited by Tivaroni, *op. cit*. vol. iii.

Over Lombardy Radetzky ruled with a rod of iron. He declared martial law and levied a contribution of some twenty million *francs* on a few rich Milanese: one million two hundred thousand from Pompeo Litta, and eight hundred thousand *francs* apiece from Borromeo and the Princess Belgiojoso.

The confiscation of her revenues crippled the financial resources of our revolutionary heroine. Paris was out of the question; partly for reasons of economy, partly owing to the intensity of the hatred she vouchsafed the government which had decreed and consummated the Roman outrage. Later, her resentment became susceptible of politic modification; but the fires of vindictiveness burned too fiercely now to permit of compromise.

Exiled alike from home and adopted country, the princess yearned for complete dissociation from the scenes and interests which during the last twenty years had witnessed and incited unavailing material sacrifice and intellectual effort. Of the nature of the considerations which prompted her final decision we can only hazard conjectures, for of personal record there is very little. Can it have been the sensational discovery made by the Austrian authorities during a prying exploration of the princess's villa at Locate which contributed to her desire to avoid for a time the inquisitiveness of Western civilisation?

Be this as it may, Christina Belgiojoso, accompanied by her little daughter and a small suite, left Rome to embark (August 3, 1849) on the good ship *Mentone,* bound for the Orient.

CHAPTER 11

The Princess Visits Greece

With her departure from Europe ends what may be called the heroic phase of Donna Christina's life: a period, by reason of its publicity, open to varying, often hostile, criticism. Yet the subsequent career of this truly exceptional woman, hardly less fierce of purpose if lacking perhaps the brilliancy of her earlier years, is no less captivating, and certainly no more conventional in substance or surroundings.

Before accompanying our heroine on her Eastern pilgrimage, we must satisfy the reader's legitimate curiosity concerning the sensational incident which may, or may not, have influenced her decision to flee the conventionalities of European society.

While searching the princess's villa for incriminating papers wherewith to confound the unfortunate patriots who had temporarily delivered Milan out of their hands, the Austrian police discovered, in a wardrobe of the private apartments, the body of a man, clothed in black. Naturally a crime was immediately suspected; the caretaker of the villa was arrested, and an inquiry set on foot.

The body was readily recognised as that of one Gaetano Stelzi, a young collaborator of the princess's on her periodical, the *Crociato*, and as such, a frequent visitor at her house both in Milan and in the country. But according to the parish registers Gaetano Stelzi was buried in the churchyard of Locate, where he had been laid to rest in the presence of numerous witnesses on June 19, 1848! Yet there was no mistaking the identity of the corpse which confronted the terrified spectators, for it was carefully embalmed and in perfect preservation.

An investigation of the grave in the little *Campo santo* (Holy field), of the village disclosed the fact that the coffin buried there contained only a heavy log of wood. It was afterwards ascertained that Stelzi, a charming and talented man of twenty-seven, but already in the last stages of consumption, expired suddenly of a haemorrhage of the lungs in the presence of the terror-stricken princess, at her house in Milan, on June 16, 1848. For reasons unexplained, she took steps to have the body partially embalmed, although within three days the coffin was interred at Locate. But the mystery attaching to the secret transfer of the corpse to a cupboard in her villa, and to the sham funeral services held over a bit of timber, has never been solved. (Barbiera, *op. cit.*)

Barbiera evokes the memory of Spanish "Crazy Jane," who kept ever with her the remains of her well-beloved Philippe le Bel; but the Italian biographer urges that although eccentric, and afflicted with a distressing nervous malady, Donna Christina Belgiojoso was far from mad. Moreover, she was known to have a morbid horror of death, an instinctive dread of darkness, which to her peculiarly sensitive nervous organisation became peopled with ghosts and apparitions, only held at bay by the brilliant artificial illumination with which she constantly surrounded herself. This peculiarity was, however, a development of later years: there had been a time when the dim religious light of her Parisian sanctuary excited the comment of visitors.

Her share in, or cognisance of, the clandestine removal of Stelzi's body to Locate and the hideous farce of the mock burial remains un-proved. Fantastic as were her vagaries, the hypothesis that she caused the corpse to be concealed in her own house during all those weeks, and then locked in a cupboard until she should return from an ab-sence which promised to be extremely protracted, is too preposterous for serious consideration.

We can imagine, however, the scandal the gruesome affair created in Milan and Paris. Here, indeed, was a choice morsel to roll on the tongue of a perfidious friend or an avowed enemy; and the princess had many of both. We may be sure the details of this sensational dis-covery lost nothing of their lurid colouring when transmitted to Paris and circulated from mouth to mouth by the *habitués* of the *salons* where her undeniable beauty, her haughty reserve, and sometimes un-comfortable originality had left many a heart-burn and excited many a jealousy. Callous as she habitually showed herself to the world's es-timate, it would be hardly surprising if she shrank from personal ex-posure to the malicious slander which the grim disclosure at Locate must inevitably arouse.

Moreover, the experiences through which she had lately passed both in Milan and in Rome had profoundly discouraged her. Some-one has said that the collected experience of today destroys the illusions of yesterday and darkens the prospect of tomorrow. Politically, perhaps socially also, the princess had been brought to a forcible recognition of the truth contained in this pessimistic aphorism. Apparently dissimilar as were the two occasions on which her ideals had seemed on the way to realisation, first at Milan and then in Rome—the ideal Monarchical and the ideal Republican, both democratic in their genesis—the fundamental principle and purpose had been identical: Political Liberty and National Independence. The experiences collected had in both cases ruthlessly destroyed illusions and darkened prospects. Her intellectual as well as her physical energies demanded a period of restorative quiescence.

The impulsively passionate phase of her political activity was indeed over: the apex of her patriotic fervency was reached in Rome. Although we shall find her pen as industrious, her literary output as prolific, as of yore, yet the old ring of defiant protest will have yielded to the subtler pleadings of persuasive argument. Henceforth she mingles with the audience, at most occasionally prompter and critic to the actors holding the political stage, or filling minor parts in the great National Drama of which she was privileged to witness the apotheosis, as she had the opening scenes.

From Rome, the princess journeyed to Malta, and thence continued her voyage to Greece. The physical and mental lassitude which possessed her benumbed the intellectual enjoyment the contemplation of the classic scenes around her might have been expected to evoke. She herself recognised and sadly records this unaccustomed inability to appreciate the influences which deeply affected one of her companions on the Plain of Marathon. She writes:

> This man, well read and intelligent though he was, possessed a nature far more positive than poetic. Yet I saw a tear on his cheek: while I, be it confessed to my shame, all I felt during that visit to Marathon was that the day was very warm.—*Asie Mineure et Syrie.*

This numbing of emotional impulse was intermittent. The world and its many interests were still of deep moment to her. If the heroism of Themistocles and his gallant band failed to stir her enthusiasm, the political and social decadence of the modern Greek, and his apparent ingratitude towards the friends of 1821, excited her indignation and scathing criticism.

In her letters to the *National* of Paris, written from Athens, she makes insinuations and draws conclusions which raise a very hornet's nest about her ears. One of Vieusseux's correspondents, (Vieusseux Correspondence. National Library, Florence), writing on October 18, 1850, exclaims:

> I can find no words to express the exasperation produced among the Greeks by those letters of the Belgiojoso's to the *National* of Paris.

In truth, the princess was attacked with the utmost virulence by the Greek press, even the most moderate journals, and those whose editors she had counted among her friends, joining in the general hue and cry. Vieusseux's correspondent continues:

> The friends of the Belgiojoso should urge her to retract: otherwise, also on account of what she has said concerning the Romans, her reputation will be lost in the opinion of all.

It is possible that Athens became too hot for the audacious critic, whose fingers thus mercilessly rubbed salt into the raw spots of an intensely susceptible national pride. At any rate, we next hear of her in Constantinople, where she makes a considerable, although uneventful, stay, preparatory to crossing over into Asia Minor; there to lead an existence in many respects similar to that of Lady Hester Stanhope.

Concerning the circumstances which prompted the pitching of her tent in the Anatolian vale of Ciaq-Maq-Oglon, the princess tells us that as soon as it became known that a lady, exiled from her own country, desired to find a resting-place in the neighbourhood, offers of estates which their owners were disposed to part with poured in. The property which finally tempted her lay midway between Scutari on the eastern shore of the Bosphorus and Angora, four or five days' march from either.

"Of course I was considered an easy prey," says the princess; "and perhaps I was." However, as she paid but five thousand *francs* for a valley "about two leagues long by a third of a league in width, intersected by a river, framed in wooded mountains, with a house, a mill, and a saw-mill," the bargain sounds fair enough. When the purchase price was noised about, however, the countryside opened wide its eyes, and acknowledged that the heirs of the late owner had made *un coup de filet étourdissant*. But as these same heirs proved friendly, and their protection was of incalculable value in such a lonely region, the princess felt herself amply compensated thereby for the difference between the market value of her estate and the fancy price she had paid.

A letter dated from her new abode August 13, 1851, addressed to her sister-in-law, the Marchesa Visconti d'Aragona, and published by Signer Barbiera, furnishes interesting details of her new venture. Home-sickness claims the lonely expatriate in the opening paragraphs of her epistle: recollections of her half-brother's luxurious villa on Lake Maggiore, mind-pictures of the beloved Italian landscape, crowd her weary brain, she sighs:

> *Chi sa!* Perhaps God holds in reserve for me a more quiet and serene old age than has been vouchsafed my youth; and if my strength holds out, if I can so order this place that my presence is no longer necessary to make it produce the promised fruits, I shall not delay revisiting Europe. . . .

And then she affords a glimpse of some of the reasons which urged the unusual step she has taken.

> Of myself, and of my plans I have not yet spoken, although you express the desire to know them. I will tell you, therefore, that reduced to sore pecuniary straits as I am, owing to many sacrifices, to fines, to exactions, to taxation, &c., I thought I ought to take advantage of an opportunity which offered for the future, or rather promised Maria some probability of fortune. I therefore bought for five thousand *francs* an estate which in Europe would be a duchy: good, very fertile land, partly valley, partly hill and mountain, irrigated by a river and by numerous canals. The purchase of cattle, of agricultural implements, the construction of a house, of stables, granary, hay-lofts, &c., cost a little more than the land itself; but although I have been here nearly a year, what with my acquisitions, running expenses, and the maintenance of a numerous household, I have not yet spent twenty thousand *francs*. You see, therefore, that the outlay has been small.
>
> As to the returns which I hope to derive from this property, I don't know why they should be much inferior to those it would produce if situated in Europe, because from here to Constantinople the merchandise is transported at small expense in four or five days, and in Constantinople all kind of produce is sold as in Europe. I have, for instance, rice-fields like yours; and rice costs here about the same as in Milan. For the present, I intend cultivating only the valley; but if in time I succeed in

covering my hills with vines, the profits may be immense.

The garnered atavisms of generations of Lombard landowners now stood the princess in good stead. As among her Locate peasants, so amidst the unfamiliar associates of a Turkish farm she found scope for the energies ever battling within her. Even the maternal instinct, so conspicuously absent, or dormant, during the earlier years, would seem to have been awakened. She continues:

> But how better employ the years of exile, than in preparing for my daughter a source of future ease? . . . I congratulate myself, then, on the resolution I have embraced; and I trust that my sacrifices will not be without fruit. In the meanwhile, Maria enjoys it. To see her so robust and so happy is for me the greatest consolation.

The only allusion to the distressing political situation at home would appear to lie in the somewhat ambiguous phrase with which she closes:

> Since thinking of the happiness of those I love is one of my principal comforts, so would I fain know whether the results of the past agitations have been obliterated.—Extract from unpublished letter quoted by Barbiera, *op. cit.*

This would seem to imply that the princess was in ignorance whether her relations and others implicated in the insurrection were still subjected to the fines, confiscations, or petty persecutions with which Radetzky inaugurated the reversion to Austrian tyranny. Two years have elapsed since the princess left Rome, three since the collapse of the Provisional Government of Lombardy, but barely a twelvemonth since she sought her rustic retreat. News travelled slowly in Anatolia; the means of intercommunication were elementary and at best uncertain, as witness the futile attempts of her relatives to forward funds—perhaps letters shared the same fate; which would account for lapses frequent and extensive in her knowledge of current public affairs in Europe.

Farming and the administrative details connected with her property did not, however, occupy all the princess's leisure. An indefatigable worker and a close observer, she threw herself with her accustomed vigour into the study of the social and economic phenomena of her new environment. Lifting boldly the curtain veiling Turkish family life, she penetrated the dark recesses of the *harem*, often carrying a gleam of light to the human cattle lethargically ruminating midst surroundings at once repulsive and pathetic.

This "Queen" from an unknown world, radiant with the effulgence of an untasted and wholly incomprehensible liberty, both awed and captivated the slaves whose squalid luxury and foul enclosures she has described with characteristic candour. Possessing, as we know, the pen of a ready writer, such incursions were rapidly and graphically chronicled, appearing later in various English, French, and American periodicals. The *Revue des Deux Mondes* continued to open its austere columns to her prose for many years, most of the chapters of her book, *Asia Minor and Syria*, (published in 1858), having originally enjoyed the hospitality of the famous French review.

Commonplace as many of the impressions and appreciations must appear to us today, when the ease and frequency of communication have tarnished the glamour of Eastern life, and shorn it of much of the mystery which constituted its chief charm, we can yet turn over the four hundred and odd pages of this still very readable work with an interest not merely perfunctory.

The journey which the book describes would, indeed, be a very venturesome one today. Leaving her quiet home at Ciaq-Maq-Oglon in January, 1852, the princess, accompanied by her daughter and a small following, which included for a part of the trip the younger brother of the late owners of her estate, travelled on horseback across Asia Minor to Jerusalem, where she arrived in the spring. A prolonged stay and extensive excursions having been made in Syria, the return journey was undertaken by another route, the party reaching the Anatolian farm in safety after an absence of eleven months.

Her style is easy, the narrative flowing, and although here and there we are confronted with descriptions of manners and usages, or dry dissertations on religious practices, wearisome because so familiar to us today, the adventurous nature of the expedition and its many and stirring incidents amply compensate for the time devoted to the perusal of her book. We scan its pages with the secret hope of surprising some illusive trait of the complex personality of the authoress who torments and stimulates our curiosity as much by reason of what is apparent as of that which we suspect in unfathomed depths.

And, indeed, our patience is not unrewarded. Here and there, unconsciously doubtless, the princess drops a corner of the veil. Now and again through the obscuring mists of romanticism and artificiality which weave her cloak of "pose," she stands revealed in unaffected simplicity, failing which our sympathy would be inevitably withheld. These touches of naturalness become more frequent with the prolongation of her sojourn amidst simple and primitive surroundings, with a people whose social instincts contrast so radically with the ethics of the civilisation in which it has been her ambition to hold a conspicuous place. We are conscious of a broader conception, a wider tolerance of things spiritual and material; and with it, unavoidably perhaps, a corresponding attenuation of the fiery enthusiasms of the militant period.

As at Marathon, so in Jerusalem. Within the Holy Places the authoress of the *Essai sur la Fondation du Dogme catholique* (Essay on the Catholic Dogma Foundation) pleads herself insentient to the emotional mysticism popularly attaching thereto. Before the panorama of Nazareth, this inability to place herself in reverential harmony with the spiritual ambient acutely distresses her.

" . . . It was in vain that I evoked the great memories of the Bible and the Gospels: nothing succeeded in awakening in me that enthusiasm which so many choice spirits had felt when in presence of the same sites. Humiliated and discouraged, I went to seek the Capuchin father charged with doing the honours of Nazareth for me."—*Asie Mineure et Syrie*.

Yet she enters "this region consecrated by the adoration of all ages," animated with a keen sense of expectancy. She regrets at first that her arrival took place at night: a few hours later she congratulates herself on having done so, thus retarding "a painful and singular affliction" or "*l'impuissance de tirer de la vue réelle des lieux célèbres les émotions que m'en procure en quelque sorte la vite intérieure et anticipée*" We have preferred to leave the last phrase in the original, fearing to disturb with an English rendering its subtle psychological aroma. In a measure, the words lay bare the anomalous intellectual scepticism which stamps the princess's religious and secular enthusiasms, forcing us (sometimes with a sense of shame, as for an injustice done) to ask ourselves, "Was she ever sincere?" Yet who shall say she was not? She was an *exaltée*; intellectually at once a sceptic and a mystic. As it was with historical sites, so it was throughout her life with political theories. For the abstruse—the Ideal—her enthusiasms burned fiercely, and no sacrifice was too great for the attainment of her aim: yet disillusion invariably followed on a closer view.

In spite of the discouragement experienced at Nazareth, she spends the first night of the sojourn in Jerusalem, *la ville du Christ*, in "serene meditation." But as she visits the various Biblical sites she makes no secret of her substantial doubts as to the authenticity of the sacred topography.

After a month in Jerusalem the princess and her friends visited the Dead Sea and the Jordan. Ensconced in a shady nook by the sacred stream, divested of all but indispensable clothing, a book by her hand and the fragrant *narghilé* between her lips, she prepares for meditation. It was hot, and the princess was tired and drowsy. Despite her elaborate preparations, the historic surroundings are conducive to no more transcendental rhapsody than a common place:

> What memories are awakened on the banks of the Jordan! What scenes! What images are evoked at the mere mention of the name!

True, her meditation is rudely disturbed by the report of firearms and a languid interest in the ensuing scrimmage between her escort and the members of a rival Bedouin tribe. Yet even under more tranquil circumstances must not that emotional *impuissance*, when brought face to face with the reality of historic sites, have precluded a more eloquent outburst? Music alone, aside from politics, was capable of inspiring mental exaltation. Although undoubtedly a religious woman, her emotional cravings no longer found solace in the extravagant devotion which had soothed her in her earlier years. But by music she was not unfrequently moved to an hysterical state conducive to religious ecstasy. She has herself confessed to being excited to such religious fervour through the agency of the great Mario's sublime voice that, like the Christian martyrs of old, she would willingly have faced the ravenous beasts of the arena.

Of the ecstatic rapture of mysticism and the austere contentment of the ascetic she had tasted during the composition of her recondite *Essay on the Formation of the Catholic Dogma*, surrounding at that period her material life with all the spiritual adjuncts the solemnity of her theme suggested. Although such phases were transitory, they were temperamental, and accordingly to be looked for in any emotional crisis. The phenomenon of their non-occurrence amidst scenes usually most calculated to provoke vivid impressions would seem to demonstrate a species of psychic reaction or atrophy, induced, perhaps, by a prolonged period of quiescence in the nervous malady from which she was a sufferer.

But if her journey was not fruitful in emotions of the soul, it offered every variety of physical distraction and excitement.

As we peruse her volume we stand aghast at the temerity of the expedition she had undertaken, while we marvel at the pluck and physical endurance displayed in the face of frequent and serious danger and of continual discomfort and fatigue. Her horses are stricken with a mysterious, mortal disease; her escort mutinies and deserts her; she is surrounded at times by murderers and brigands, and always by knaves of less heroic stamp. Hunger and thirst, cold and overpowering heat she meets all alike with unfailing cheerfulness and philosophic resignation, but also, on occasion, with a determination which staggers those who attempt to influence or coerce her. On being grossly insulted by a band of passing Arabs, she is prompted to retaliate and demand satisfaction for a gratuitous affront. She writes:

I had, fortunately, that day placed a copy of *Don Quixote* in my saddle-bag, and I only needed to cast my eyes on Cervantes' ironical romance in order to recover my calm.

Again, on the road to Damascus, a native, acting for the nonce as British Consul, strongly dissuades the selection of a certain route well known to be infested by brigands, she, the while, gently persisting in the maintenance of her original plan. In despair of overcoming her determination, the harassed official exclaims with a subtle irony not unworthy of the Spaniard aforementioned:

You are right. When one places one's confidence in God so strongly as you would appear to do, one has nothing to fear from the wicked. Choose whatever road you will, *Madame*; you may fall in with brigands, they may maltreat your body, but they will be powerless to prevent the repose of your soul in God.

Notwithstanding the ill-concealed pessimism of this harangue, the undaunted princess, with great difficulty inspiring her escort with a modicum of her own superabundant confidence, travels safely over the dangerous territory with only a false alarm in the dead of night to break the monotony of the sandy waste.

But as the story of her adventures fills a thick volume, we cannot transcribe them in detail here. Suffice it to record that our intrepid heroine penetrated regions practically as little known and untrodden today as when she traversed them over half a century ago. Leaving the Mediterranean behind her, she struck out from Adana to Tarsus and Koniah; thence over the arid territory of the Kurds, midway between

Kara-Hissar and Angora, towards the Black Sea.

There is a note of quiet content in her description of the home-coming—when first they catch sight of the peaceful vale, shimmering in the sunshine, as they rein in their horses on the brow of the hill above.

> Of a certainty, it was not a return to my own country, to the house of my ancestors, or the familiar surroundings of child-hood and youth. But after so long a journey through unknown lands, 'mid social conditions so different from those I had hith-erto experienced, it was something to be able to say to myself, 'This house belongs to me; my bread will be harvested in those fields; these labourers are attached to me, if not by affection, at least by interest.' Exiled to a foreign land, I found myself, after eleven months' absence, in the spot where exile was for me robbed of some of its bitterness. . . . . I brought back with me all I held dearest; myself the worse for neither privations nor fatigue, and with a vast store of memories. Here was subject for rendering fervent thanksgiving to the Lord. With this purpose I shut myself in my chamber, but could find no more eloquent words than these: 'Thank Thee, my God, thank Thee.'—*Asie Mineure et Syrie.*

CHAPTER 12

The Princess Decides to Return to Europe

It was in December, 1852, that the princess again took up her abode at Ciaq-Maq-Oglon. Her long absence was not calculated to improve the prospects of a speedy financial return from her Asiatic investment. On the contrary, from one cause or another, but principally from lack of supervision by the mistress, the farm proved a pecuniary loss, hardly producing the bare necessaries of life for her family and those dependent on her. To eke out a modest pittance, mother and daughter now bent over their embroidery frames, disposing of their work in the bazaars of Constantinople. The pages of foreign reviews and periodicals, moreover, afforded the princess some remuneration for accounts of her recent experiences in the remote districts through which she had travelled.

While sitting at her desk one calm morning, a ferocious and dastardly attempt was made upon her life by one of her own household. It would appear that the servant, an Italian who had accompanied the princess to Asia Minor, had recently received his discharge, ostensibly for repeated misconduct, but perhaps also owing to the pressing economical crisis. Furious over dismissal, the servant stole up behind her and attacked his mistress with a dagger, inflicting seven wounds.

The princess was only saved from certain death by the timely arrival of her daughter, who put the assassin to flight before he could execute his fiendish design. Fortunately, none of the wounds were fatal, although one received in the neck left permanent traces, causing her to hold her head bent forward; while another, in the breast, occasioned at times considerable oppression of the respiratory organs. For a time, however, her condition was critical, for isolated as were

VICTOR EMMANUEL II.

her surroundings, the princess could procure no medical aid. Her indomitable pluck, together with the knowledge of surgery acquired in Rome, helped her through the painful crisis, and enabled her gradually to overcome both the physical and moral shock, with the exception of the permanent results just mentioned.

But as the months dragged on she became increasingly convinced that her agricultural venture was doomed to financial failure. Perhaps, also, the disquieting news she received from home concerning the results of Mazzini's unpardonable folly in fomenting the Milanese rising of February 6, 1853, determined her to make what disposition she could of her Anatolian property and yield to the entreaty of her relatives that she should return to Europe and permit them to seek a remedy for her temporary pecuniary embarrassments.

After all, the investment, financially unprofitable though it was, had served a distinct purpose in affording her a peaceful haven of refuge during this period of exile, and especially in contributing by its restful isolation towards the recovery of that mental calm and intellectual balance seriously menaced by the harrowing scenes of the drama in which she had taken so active a part. It could be in no way derogatory to her personal dignity to accept the assistance offered by her relatives. Besides, since the failure of her farm to provide a living, she had little choice in the matter, for, by a proclamation of February 18, 1853, the Austrian Emperor again sequestrated the fortunes of the Lombard exiles.

To what extent her resources were crippled we have no means of accurately ascertaining: yet it would not appear that absolute poverty accompanied the motley following with which the princess landed at Marseilles during this same year, 1853. With Donna Christina penury had always been a relative term. Even in the days when Monsieur Thiers exercised his culinary gifts in the preparation of those historic omelets in her Parisian garret, there is reason to believe that the princess disposed of larger revenues than it suited her mood to admit. On the present occasion, the bankrupt exile's train included, besides her daughter Maria, an English governess, two Turkish men-servants, an Arab steed, four huge Asiatic hounds, and two long-tailed Angora cats. (Barbiera, *op. cit.*)

Accompanied by her heterogeneous belongings, the princess took up her temporary abode under the hospitable roof of her half-sister Theresa, who had become the wife of a Frenchman, the Marquis Charles d'Aragona.

Christina Belgiojoso was, as we know, decidedly out of love with Mazzini's inflexible creed. Her Roman experiences had shown her the seamy side of his idealism along with its seductive qualities. Like Manin, Pallavicino, and other erstwhile Republicans, her ambitions for Italy soared above party or dynastic interests, and flew straight at the expulsion of the foreigner and the attainment, at all costs, of National Unity. The form of government was a secondary consideration. With Manin she cried to young Victor Emmanuel:

Make Italy and we are with you: if not, we must look elsewhere.

The futility of unorganised, spasmodic insurrection, of demoralising local agitation along the old Mazzinian lines, as contrasted with the programme which Cavour was patiently advocating, had become convincingly apparent to the saner patriots. "*Revolution through evolution*" may be said to have been Cavour's maxim at this period. Mazzini held the reverse to be correct. Of the two, the first seemed to offer the more serious guarantees of success and stability, and the less headstrong and impetuous elements of Italian patriotism throughout the Peninsula were already accepting the theories of rigorous discipline and moderation enjoined by the Piedmontese statesmen.

Not so, however, Mazzini or the remnant of his following in Lombardy which preserved intact and uncontaminated the immutable traditions handed down since the founding of "Young Italy" twenty odd years before. In Milan, Brescia, Mantua, and a dozen smaller towns, these irreconcilable fanatics kept up their lodges. Mazzini held the threads of these affiliations more or less tightly in his hands; manipulating and counselling their local chiefs from his headquarters in London.

In Lombardy, the social conditions had changed but little during the last five years. The Nationalist spirit survived, in spite of the brutality of systematic repression. Austrian officers and civil servants were rigorously boycotted in society; and even in the theatres and other popular resorts a distinct line was drawn between oppressor and oppressed. There was no semblance of fusion; in fact, violent collisions between civilians and arrogant officials were of daily occurrence, serving to fan the flames of exasperation on the one side and deadly hatred on the other.

By an accident the ever-vigilant police stumbled upon the clue to a seditious conspiracy in Mantua, and wholesale arrests followed. An Italian student of historical undercurrents, Professor G. Mondaini, has

HENRICH HEINE

recently published a curious account of this far-reaching conspiracy which aimed not only at insurrection in Lombardy, but plotted the assassination of Napoleon III. and the establishment of a Republic in France. (*Memorie del colonnello Majocchi, Bollettino della Società pavese di storia patria,* March, 1906.) Five of the leaders of the original conspiracy met death on the scaffold at Mantua. Their trial had been "a horrible parody of justice": it was, in fact, a repetition of the mental tortures inflicted on the unhappy *Federati* during the famous trial of 1821; but to moral coercion was now added the physical degradation of flogging and partial starvation as a means of eliciting damaging confessions.

Maddened by the barbarities practised on the persons of his fellow-conspirators, and without stopping to gauge the worth of the grossly exaggerated reports which reached him concerning the country's preparedness for successful revolt, Mazzini incited his Lombard followers to take up arms and repeat the glorious episode of 1848. Rarely has a responsible leader been guilty of a greater folly. There existed no cohesion, and but an ill-defined half-understanding among the conspirators themselves, while the movement, essentially Republican, could hope for but scant sympathy from a large majority of Lombard patriots who, eager though they were for the encouragement of the Nationalist spirit, had incorporated their interests with those of monarchical Piedmont.

The rising of February 6th was strangled at its birth, but old Radetzky proved merciless in his vengeance, and execution followed execution. To the Marshal's initiative was also due the Imperial edict which placed a fresh embargo on the property of all Lombards who had left the State for political motives, whether or no they had had any hand in the late abortive insurrection.

Thus, it was that the Princess Belgiojoso, in the distant seclusion of her Oriental valley, found herself once more between the far-reaching talons of the double-headed eagle, from whose ferocity she had so frequently and so greatly suffered.

Her old friend Heinrich Heine would appear to have exerted what influence he possessed with Thiers, Guizot, and other French statesmen, urging them to make such unofficial representations at Vienna as might result in the raising of the embargo on the princess's Italian property. The Princess della Rocca asserts that her uncle, Heine, was successful in his self-imposed mission, and that within two years Donna Christina was not only in possession of her revenues, but had obtained permission to revisit Italy. (*Souvenirs de la Vie intime de Henri Heine.*) On the other hand, Signor Barbiera is convinced that such was not the case, and maintains that the embargo on the princess's property was raised on December 2, 1856, or on the same date as the property of all other Lombard exiles was liberated by Imperial proclamation. (Barbiera, *op. cit.*)

However, this may be, the fact remains that poor Heine, now a hopeless cripple condemned to torturing immobility, did very earnestly exert himself to alleviate his "Divinity's" material embarrassments, and obtain the abrogation of the ban of exile which began to weigh so heavily.

Meanwhile Donna Christina was only too content to prolong her visit with her devoted half-sister Theresa. It will be remembered that the princess's mother, left a widow when barely twenty years of age, took as her second husband the Marquis Alexander Visconti d'Aragona. By this marriage there were several children, and of these Theresa was the eldest girl. Her gentle, plastic nature presented a striking contrast to that of her imperious half-sister, at the shrine of whose brilliant personality she worshipped in secret.

In a few simple lines, she has sketched this childish subjugation, which lasted throughout her life. She notes on the pages of her diary:

> I have always loved my sister Christina. When I was a girl she dazzled me with her intelligence; and I thought myself transported to a fairy realm when she, fourteen years my senior (I was then seven), permitted me to spend a day in her rooms looking over engravings and learning French. My sister left Italy shortly after her marriage, and for many years I saw her no more. In 1836, I found her again in Paris, in her attractive house in the Rue d'Anjou, surrounded by illustrious men, and receiving her numerous friends. She desired to keep me near her, and persuaded my mother to arrange a marriage for me in France. And, indeed, I married on October 15, 1837 (the Feast-day of my Patron Saint); but my mother, alas! was no longer with me. I had had the grief of losing her two months earlier.—Quoted by Barbiera, *op. cit.*

To the purely sentimental longings of this gentle soul the passionate enthusiasm of her sister's patriotism, with its political complexities, was frankly incomprehensible. Yet she too loved her Italy—loved it for its colour and subtle and illusive charm, for "the artistic atmosphere

165

everywhere diffused," its pictures, its music: while her countrymen themselves appealed to her innate refinement owing to "the gentleness of their ways, the delicacy of their instincts, the simplicity of their social intercourse." (*Diary of Marchesa Charles d'Aragona.*)

Strong as were the bonds of mutual affection between these two daughters of the same mother, their point of view was too dissimilar to allow of intellectual sympathy. Nevertheless, Donna Christina, while maintaining her moral ascendency, was deeply sensible of her sister's simple devotion, appreciating with all her heart the restful domestic solicitude so unstintedly accorded. As she writes to her half-brother, Albert Visconti d'Aragona:

> When one has troubles great as mine one feels the urgent need of clinging to the affections of one's childhood, which are the most faithful of all; while the ties of blood, which cannot be dissolved, appear as the most trusty protection. Happy then are they who find among relations and friends both upright minds and sincere and affectionate hearts.—Barbiera, *op. cit.*

CHAPTER 13

More Intrigues

Yet, notwithstanding the attractions of family life the princess was moved to revisit Paris. Her resentment against the government which had countenanced the annihilation of the Roman Republic had cooled. The man who now sat on the Imperial throne of France was master of the situation; and he had promised her in days gone by that when his hour of triumph came he would not be forgetful of Italy.

The cunning brain of Cavour was already at work shaping the destinies of Piedmont, which he was among the first to realise could be materially advanced by making an ally of the author of the *coup d'état*. The dispute between the Latin and Orthodox Churches over the Holy Places in Palestine, resulting in the Crimean War, afforded Cavour the opportunity he coveted. By securing a seat in the Congress of Paris, he could officially give vent to his country's lament concerning the maladministration of Austria's Italian provinces.

To the princess's chastened zeal the spread of the principles which regulated the working of the National Society, at once Unitarian and Royalist in its scope, inspired renewed confidence. Two men of staunch patriotism stood at the head of this League—Daniel Manin, dictator of the Venetian Republic of 1849, and the Marquis George Pallavicino-Trivulzio, the conspirator of 1821, and martyr of Spielberg fame. The latter was a cousin of Donna Christina, and had, moreover, been intimately associated with her stepfather in those dark days when her childish patriotism had been awakened through the anguish of suspense which for so many months hung over her home.

Pallavicino was at this time (1853-54) an ardent advocate of Cavour's policy of alliances, especially of that with France; and although erratic and often inexcusably independent, his services were for many years greatly appreciated. An indefatigable scribe, he plied his pen in the Liberal cause, many French, English, and Belgian periodicals gladly welcoming his able essays. With Mazzini, he had no more patience than our heroine, although he would at one time gladly have won him over to membership in the National Society. The *marquis's* large income, like his cousin Belgiojoso's, had been reduced to a bare pittance by the sequestration of his Lombard interests: yet he refused pecuniary assistance from friends abroad, (*Memorie*, vol. iii.), and practically supported himself by his pen. An ardent admirer and valued counsellor of Garibaldi, he was called, in 1860, to Naples as Pro-Dictator, and by his loyalty, moderation, and firmness at a perilously critical juncture prevented the enactment of what must inevitably have proved an irretrievable political disaster. (Whitehouse, *Collapse of the Kingdom of Naples*.)

The Paris which the Princess Belgiojoso revisited in 1854 presented a very different social aspect from the capital of Louis Philippe, or even the short-lived Republic. Some of the salons had been closed by death, while others timidly held their doors ajar, uncertain whether to welcome the new *régime* or to sulk. There was as yet faint promise of that dazzling intellectual and material brilliancy which was to symbolise the reign of Napoleon and Eugenie.

The faithful Heine, dragging out an existence in which bodily torture was intensified by domestic infelicity, greeted his "divine princess" with touching rapture. But the freedom and ease of the old companionship soon withered before the blasts of ferocious conjugal jealousy which the intimacy aroused. Thierry, the blind historian, her quondam *protégée*, groping his way through physical darkness to intellectual light, was able to lay in the lap of his friend and benefactress his admirable essay on the "Third Estate." Another historian, Mignet—"*le beau Mignet*," whom rumour once designated as "*l'ami le plus tendre et le plus intime de la belle Italienne*," (J. Legras, *Henri Heine*), and who had been associated with the princess on the *National*—was still adding laurels to his literary crown. Mignet, indeed, outlived his *innamorata*, dying in 1884, at the age of eighty-eight.

De Musset's passion for the Belgiojoso had burnt itself out years before, and the embers of his fickle heart had been fanned into flame a dozen times since the memorable episode related in a former chapter. It is doubtful even that her presence awakened a reminiscent thrill in the breast of the sated libertine, who now began to seek inspiration in drink. Much water had, indeed, run under the bridges since the graceful poet playfully wrote to his trusted "Marraine" (Madame Jaubert):

It is certain that I am horribly in love, but I don't know with whom: perhaps it is with you! so I don't know how to address my note. Supposing I wrote, for instance: '*A Madame la prin Jaucesse bert de Bel rue Taitgiojoso bout*'? do you think that would reach Saint-Germain?'—Madame Jaubert, *op. cit.*

In 1854 the change in the poet's character had become noticeable to his friends; yet he preserved almost to the end (1857) the singular charm of person and wit which endeared him to his generation. "What will be the representative ideal of de Musset with posterity?" asked Madame Jaubert of the philosopher Chenavard, as the poet left them one evening.

Alfred de Musset, *Madame*, will be for all time the personification of Youth and Love.—Madame Jaubert, *op. cit.*

Under the changed conditions the princess's visit was, from a social standpoint, a series of disappointments. Although Donna Christina was only forty-six years of age, "youth and love" had flown; while she looked much older than she was. The last five years had left the stamp of suffering upon her delicate features. By the hand of the would-be assassin she lost that haughty poise of her graceful head which had lent an added dignity to her regal carriage. Even now she stooped in walking, carrying her head slightly bent; her whole bearing conveying the impression of physical lassitude, when not of actual suffering.

But if from a sentimental point of view this return to the scenes of the triumphs of her youth was full of painful deceptions, on the other hand the princess found matter for considerable encouragement in the political world, and more especially in the emperor's immediate *entourage*. At the sovereign's elbow stood Count Arese, one of Lombardy's staunchest patriots, and a lifelong friend and intimate of Napoleon's, his companion in exile and adversity, and now in the days of power and prosperity his trusted confidant. The presence of this patriot so near the person of the ex-Carbonaro, whose heart was known to favour emancipation from the foreign yoke, augured well for Italy. The undercurrents of Cavour's diplomacy were flowing steadily towards France. Towards the broadening of the channels and the formation of subtle but substantial ties the princess resolved to dedicate what energy remained to her.

Circumstances, perhaps political interest as well as private, prompted a return to Italy. From Lombardy she was still banished, but Piedmont gladly welcomed influential immigration from over the neighbouring frontier, readily granting citizenship to such as desired to throw in their lot with that of the more progressive State. Her cousin George Pallavicino, had not only taken advantage of the facilities thus extended, but was now serving his adopted country in the Sardinian Parliament. Two of her half-sisters married Piedmontese noblemen and settled in Turin, where the youngest, the Marchesa di Rorà, became the mistress of a prominent political and diplomatic salon, much frequented by Cavour.

As was to be expected, Princess Belgiojoso soon made a place for herself in Turinese political circles. By right of her exalted social position and family connections all doors were open to her. Her fame as a woman of parts, possessed of unusual culture and wide personal experience, perhaps also her reputation for an eccentric independence of character which had been the means of familiarising her with phases of life not generally within the sphere of action of the conventional *grande dame*, attracted about her a *coterie* of intellectual workers, statesmen, politicians, diplomatists, and others.

Cavour was quick to appreciate the services which might be rendered by this accomplished free-lance. Himself an assiduous frequenter of drawing-rooms, despite his manifold official duties and the incessant and confining labour necessitated by the administration under his charge, he kept himself thoroughly informed concerning the minute details of political life which found expression in half a dozen of the more representative social gatherings of the Piedmontese capital.

The busy statesman even found time for lengthy conversations with the princess outside the hours usually reserved for social distractions. These interviews, or familiar chats, frequently took place during the early morning hours, and sometimes the energetic Minister pushed as far afield as the Rorà's country house near Pinerolo. It is probable that the political future of Lombardy formed the principal theme of these discussions; incidentally, however, Cavour infused some of the enthusiasm he felt for the dynasty he served, and induced the princess to undertake her *History of the House of Savoy*.

The vague but suggestive schemes plotted by Donna Christina and her fellow-conspirator, who stooped to what often appeared the most trivial details in the preparation of his political plans, were destined in due season to bear their fruit. The role assigned to the princess, which is known in diplomatic parlance as *agent provocateur*, was not a particularly glorious one, and was attended besides with considerable risk. But none better than Cavour understood the skilful handling of the double-edged weapon which has proved the undoing of so many less adroit manipulators. Moreover, on this occasion his tool was an ideal one, while the ground on which it was to be used required but the merest scratching to assure an abundant harvest.

Meanwhile, between Turin with its social and political distractions and the home life at her half-brother's villa at Oleggio Castello, on Lake Maggiore, the princess spent peaceful if uneventful months, until a policy of conciliation having replaced the vexatious impositions and brutal repressive methods of Radetzky in Lombardy, home and fortune were again restored to her.

This change in Austria's traditional treatment of her Italian subjects in no way suited the plans of Cavour. The new era was inaugurated by the appointment to the vice-regal throne in Milan of the popular and fascinating Archduke Maximilian and his equally charming young wife, the Princess Charlotte. Both these names are now best known to history in connection with the fantastic dream of a Mexican Empire which germinated in the brain of Napoleon III.

Accompanying this signal mark of the Imperial favour came news of a liberal amnesty, free pardons, the restitution of confiscated estates, and mellifluous promises of administrative reforms. Pitiless for years, Vienna, having failed to crush, now sought to dazzle and cajole. The attitude assumed by Cavour before the Powers at the Congress of Paris, when he so passionately arraigned Austria's policy in Italy, was, perhaps, accountable for the change efface.

If so, it was not what the astute Piedmontese statesman had bargained for. From a political point of view the most barbarous measures of repression would have been preferable. Should the Lombard-Venetians allow themselves to be effectively lulled into a passive acquiescence in the existing political *régime* their apathetic unconcern must seriously compromise the cause of the Nationalists in the eyes of European diplomacy; for Cavour had eloquently described to the Congress the cat and dog life existing between Austrian officialdom and its Italian victims; and had predicted ceaseless revolt and popular unrest until the incubus was removed.

In face of the present difficulty Cavour took a leaf from Mazzini's book, and secretly urged political agitation. Thus, it came about that the princess was enrolled among his agents whose overt functions were to turn an ostentatiously deaf ear to the blandishments of the Austrian Court, and to shame others into doing likewise. In reality' their mandate went far beyond mere passive resistance to Imperial cajolery. Cavour urged Emilio Dandolo:

> Tell your friends to see to it that Milan is again placed in a state of siege! Throw stones at the sentinels: scribble '*Viva l'Italia!*' on every wall.

And he repeats the injunction to Count della Porta with added emphasis. At all costs, the emasculation of Italian patriotism must be prevented.

Into this work the Belgiojoso threw herself with the zest and the skill of the experienced conspirator. Every effort was put forth to popularise Victor Emmanuel, "*Il re galantuomo*" as he was now familiarly styled all over Italy, in recognition of his honesty and sincerity of purpose. The rules of Milanese patriotism made it incumbent on the citizens to isolate, to ostracise, the foreigner within their gates: Austrian officials, civil and military, were ever more rigorously boycotted. Yet a subtle change coloured the tone of social gatherings. A feeling of hope was in the air. Giovanni Visconti Venosta writes:

> Patriotism ceased to be sad and cast down as in preceding years; on the contrary, it became gay and more audacious.—*Ricordi di Gioventù.*

For the first time since 1848 the opera at the Scala became popular with Milanese social leaders. Opposition to everything Austrian became even more acute. The friction between Italian youths and the swaggering white-coated officers the living personification of the foreign yoke steadily assumed a significant intensity.

As of old, the movement was carried into the intellectual domain, the *Crepùscolo* taking up the work of the *Conciliatore*, suppressed in 1821. Carlo Tenca edited this organ, and among his collaborators the Princess Belgiojoso held a not insignificant place. The influence of this periodical was considerable: its tone lofty and dignified. Although following every branch of the intellectual movements of the period, artistic, scientific, and sociological, the *Crepùscolo* invariably and systematically ignored any reference to Austria. Visconti Venosta says:

> This obstinate and haughty silence, was remarked and understood by all, and constituted a more efficacious propaganda than any noisy protest, had an active protest been possible at that time (1856-1857).—Visconti Venosta, *op. cit.*

Born in the famous salon of the Countess Clara Maffei early in

1850, the *Crepùscolo* valiantly persevered with its eloquently silent and subtle propaganda during ten long years. (R. Barbiera, *Salotto de la Contessa Maffei*.) Mazzinian in its early sympathies, after 1853 it had broken with that irresponsible agitator and adopted the Cavourian programme.

When in 1857 the Austrian Emperor decided to visit his Italian dominions, Tenca was informed by the Director of Police that it would be considered incumbent on the editors of the *Crepùscolo* to make becoming reference to the advent of the gracious sovereign. Tenca replied that as his journal never occupied itself with the domestic affairs of Austria, he saw no reason for departing from established custom in the present instance. In spite of threats and coercion, he held his ground, and the *Crepùscolo* completely ignored the Imperial visit.

As a matter of fact, the visit took place amidst general constraint and social gloom. Word had been passed round that no invitations to Court functions were to be accepted, and few cared to risk the censure of public opinion such an infringement of the unwritten law must entail. In many streets through which the Imperial procession passed the blinds were drawn in spite of the energetic action of the police, who in many instances forcibly tore open the windows, hastily hanging out anything in the way of decoration they could lay hands on. (Visconti Venosta, *op. cit.*)

Christina Belgiojoso and Clara Maffei were old friends, and during the stirring times of 1848 the princess had been a frequent visitor in her *salon*. Six years younger than the princess, the Countess Clara, on her marriage with the poet Maffei, had thrown herself heart and soul into the political and literary life of Milan. For fifty-two consecutive years (1834-1886) her *salon* was the rendezvous not merely of her compatriots but of intellectual Europe. The list of celebrities who thronged her modest drawing-room rivals that of the Belgiojoso's Parisian *salon*, and includes many of the same immortal names. Daniel Stern, Balzac, Manzoni, Liszt, Verdi, and a score of others, are of international fame; but the annals of Italian patriotism, *belles-lettres* and art teem with the names of men and women who, at one time or another during that half-century of uninterrupted hospitality, sought guidance, inspiration, or intellectual entertainment among the politicians, poets, musicians, and wits who congregated round the hostess.

Although the princess on her return to Lombardy again took up her residence at Locate, her life was far from that of a recluse. She was continually either in Milan or entertaining friends from the Capital at her villa; so the social side of her existence was important. Her daughter Maria, now of an age when the attractions of society and youthful companionship appeal most forcibly, formed the pretext (if one were necessary) for the gay scenes at Locate, where a theatre was installed upon whose boards amateur actors enchanted indulgent audiences Nor did the princess herself hesitate to throw aside more serious occupations, and occasionally fill a part upon the little stage.

Much of her time was devoted, however, to the study and research necessitated by her *History of the House of Savoy*.

In her preface to this very considerable undertaking the princess frankly discloses that her object in hastening its publication is to predispose public opinion abroad to a favourable consideration of the claims and aspirations of the Piedmontese dynasty at the present political crisis. She writes:

> I was diligently prosecuting my studies into the history of the House of Savoy, and discovering each day fresh material for the belief that in a not distant future the task begun by Humbert the Saxon, and uninterruptedly continued by all his descendants, would at last be satisfactorily concluded, when the dawn of the year 1859 overtook me. Events slowly maturing during so many centuries now crowded to the fore. A hand mightier than the hand of man seemed to guide them, touching hearts, enlightening souls, inspiring with resolution the most irresolute, lending energy to the weak and will to the strong.
>
> The present head of the House of Savoy unfolded the banner of Independence and of Italian Unity, and Italy hastened to his support. But Italy needed a friend who should tender her a helping hand: God gave her France as such. Within a few days victory was on the side of right: our enemies met defeat after defeat; they were falling back upon the Alps; they were about to abandon a soil they had so long trodden with bloody feet, and in which they sowed nothing but hate, tears, or the cravings for revenge. But an obstacle, the nature of which is as yet unknown to us, suddenly rose between us and the accomplishment of our legitimate desires.
>
> An Italian province was handed over to Austria, while the power to again fetter us with the bonds of slavery was either restored or left unbroken. It was then decided to consult Europe as to the fate which was to be meted out to us. To Europe was

confided the task of determining what was best for us. We had thought to enter the haven of our desire; we found ourselves cast adrift in the open sea, exposed once more to tempest and to shipwreck.

But what did Europe want? What could she want? Could it be in her interest to perpetuate war on one of her borders, and have that strife one day affect her, and destroy her own peace? Should she not hasten, on the contrary, to extinguish that ever-burning furnace of revolution and discord which misery and oppression kept ever flaming in Italy? As it is nowadays impossible to materially destroy a nation, would it not be only natural and prudent to endeavour to transform it, making of a people hitherto an element of discord, a model of order, of practical good sense, of unity, and of progress?

Europe seems to have understood that the only means of accomplishing this transformation, of quenching this furnace of revolution, is to grant, or at least not to go contrary to, the wishes of the Italians; wishes which can be resumed as follows: fusion of the various populations, Piedmontese, Lombards, Venetians, Tuscans, &c., into one Italian Nation, and the destruction of all foreign domination.

Europe would appear to understand that, by opposing the realisation of our desires, she would perpetuate agitation in Italy, and would condemn herself to remain constantly under arms, incessantly in fear of revolutions, to find herself each day menaced with civil war and international strife. She seems to have understood all this, or at least to have suspected it, for she has refused to constitute herself our judge and the arbiter of our destiny; and, when the first step towards this unity for which we strive was accomplished, in spite of the loud threats or secret insinuations of certain Powers, she refrained from condemning us. It is to the firm and cool stand taken by Central Italy that we owe this satisfactory result. But this is only a first step towards the formation of a new Italy. In order that this first step should prove a durable conquest and should be followed by others having the same end in view, it is necessary that Europe should continue to protect us.

Now, nothing could be better calculated to ensure the continuance of this protection than the evident demonstration of the harmony of our desires with the decrees of Providence. Let

Europe become convinced concerning this harmony, and she will cease to regard the achievement of our wishes with mistrust and anxiety.

Such are the reflections which have prompted me to gather up in all haste my notes, to bind them together as best I could, and to publish them without delay. Even if I considered myself able to sway the minds of others by the sole strength of my reasoning, I would at least in common prudence dissimulate such pretence. But my arguments are only facts, and I confine myself to relating these facts. If they have not already produced the impression I expect of them, it is because they are not generally known. The history of the House of Savoy is, in truth, as unknown as a whole as in detail, and the reason for this ignorance is the insignificant size of the states subject to the descendants of Humbert the Saxon.

The history of small states presents but slight interest to readers beyond their narrow frontiers. General interest is only just beginning to be awakened in the Sardinian states; and it is only a few years ago that none would have presumed to prophecy for the House of Savoy a more brilliant future than that of the House of Este or of the Bourbons of Naples. Since events have begun to dispel the cloud which enveloped the destinies of this noble and ancient House, these very happenings have left but small leisure to those who would fain devote themselves to historical research.

Should this simple account of the facts relating to the House of Savoy, of the development of its power and of its character, produce on some few minds the same impression they have on me; should the reader, after having followed the course of so many noble lives, draw from this recital the same conclusions which seem to me but natural deductions; then indeed shall I consider that the aim of my labour has been attained. . . . . —*Histoire de la Maison de Savoie*

The authoress, as she makes known in the opening paragraphs of her preface, found herself constrained to interrupt her researches and to transform her work into one of compilation. Her early purpose had been far more ambitious from the student's point of view, and she proposes to return to her subject in a more analytical spirit on some future occasion. In the present work there is no attempt at critical writing, her purpose being to lay before the reader a rapid and comprehensive panorama of historical incidents. In this she has most admirably succeeded, but of necessity at the sacrifice of those personal appreciations which, given our desire to penetrate the individual feelings of the authoress, would have afforded interesting study. Starting with the legendary and mythical surroundings of Humbert of the White Hands (1003), the princess carries her reader through the eight centuries of vicissitudes which befell this sturdy House as Counts, Dukes, and Kings, to the Peace of Villafranca (1859), "*paix mystérieuse et encore inexpliquée,*" "mysterious and unexplained peace." (*Histoire de la Maison de Savoie.*

The closing chapters, dealing with the reigns of Charles Felix, Charles Albert, and the first ten years of the rule of Victor Emmanuel II., of all of which she had herself been a witness, or at least a contemporary, are lacking in perspective, and, skeleton though they are in substance, are unavoidably tinged with sentiment. Far more elaborate studies on the same subject have since appeared, but to the general reader seeking a cursory yet eminently reliable chronicle of those romantic early centuries when the Lords of Savoy were patiently building up the noble inheritance of today, the Princess Belgiojoso's volume will still prove a source of profit and pleasure.

The book, delayed from one cause or another, was published in Paris in 1860. Its success was considerable and durable, a new edition being reprinted as lately as 1878.

CHAPTER 14

War-Clouds

Meanwhile the ardently evoked war-clouds were rolling up over the horizon, giving promise of the fruits of Cavour's long and patient diplomacy. It is unnecessary to enter here on a protracted description of the events which led up to the declaration of war between Austria and Piedmont. For the last three years all had recognised it to be inevitable. The work of the National Society, which since the death of Manin in 1857 was practically under the control of Pallavicino, was largely accountable for the spread of the war-spirit so zealously fostered by Cavour.

On their side, the Lombards sturdily refused to be dazzled by the cajolery or the really broad and liberal personal policy exercised by the young Archduke Maximilian—a policy which for a time caused Cavour and the Nationalists grave concern. After all, as Manzoni said, the Austrians only gave them "the choice of being fried or boiled." Thus, the archduke's reforms met with no gratitude: even his disinterestedness was questioned, for rumour had it that, egged on by his ambitious wife, Maximilian cradled hopes of an independent Italian crown. (Bonfadini, *Mezzo secolo*.) In Austria his concessions were considered too liberal and the home government, inspired by the military party, soon began putting obstacles in his way. Successive Imperial decrees from Vienna aimed serious blows at the social and economic fabric in Lombardy.

The most abhorrent to the lower orders was the extension of conscription, with the concomitant prohibition to those coming within its provisions to marry before the age of twenty-three. Vienna could not have played more efficiently into the hands of the Nationalists, for this act brought alien despotism directly home to the peasant, whose stolid political apathy had been impervious to the finer distinctions of patriotism, and who was rarely a revolutionist. Protests and demonstrations again became the order of the day, reviving in Milan the spirit of unrest which perpetually hovered over the city, and was rapidly spreading throughout the country districts.

Meanwhile Cavour met the Emperor Napoleon at Plombières (July, 1858), and secured his promise that an early opportunity would be made for a combined attack on Austria. (Details see *Lettere di Cavour*, iii.) Five months later (January 1, 1859) the Emperor addressed to the Austrian Envoy at Paris words which left little doubt as to the gravity of the diplomatic tension existing between the two Empires. (Hübner, *Souvenirs*, vol. ii.) As has been related in these pages, the diplomatist to whom Napoleon III. intimated his warning was that same Count Hùbner who, surprised by the "Five Days" of 1848, long lay concealed in Milan, and whose disparaging criticism of the Princess Belgiojoso's Neapolitan contingent has been recorded in a previous chapter.

A few days after the emperor's oracular remark to Hübner, Victor Emmanuel, in his speech at the opening of Parliament, significantly informed an expectant world that "he was not insensible of the cry of woe which reached him from so many parts of Italy."

In a twinkling Lombardy was ablaze. During a performance of Bellini's opera *Norma* at the Scala of Milan, the whole house joined the singers in the inspiriting chorus, "*Guerra! Guerra!*" "War! War!" shouted the enormous audience, leaping to its feet and frantically waving small tricolour flags. "War! War!" reciprocated the Austrian officers. (Visconti Venosta, *op. cit.*) For a time pandemonium reigned supreme. But popular enthusiasm was not content with mere hostile demonstrations: a vast and ever-increasing tide of fugitive military emigration set in towards Piedmont, where Garibaldi welcomed the volunteers.

The Nationalist Committees, of which the princess was so energetic a member, redoubled their propaganda, fanning the flames of the discontent kindled by the late conscription laws, and encouraging its victims to join the ranks of the liberating forces across the frontier. Provocation followed on provocation: but still Napoleon hesitated and held back. Without him Cavour dared not move. Relief from an unbearable tension finally came in April (1859) in the form of a diplomatic blunder on the part of Austria, whose representative at Turin presented a humiliating ultimatum, demanding disarmament within three days.

The responsibility of disturbing the peace of Europe was shifted to Austria, and with the wildest exultation Piedmont indignantly repudiated the right of her arrogant neighbour to meddle in her affairs. On April 26th Cavour notified Count Buol, the Austrian Chancellor, that his terms were unacceptable, and three days later France declared war on Austria.

The Princess Belgiojoso betook herself to Paris shortly before the breaking out of hostilities, charged, it was said, with a secret mission, the details of which have not been divulged. She returned to Milan after the battle of Magenta and again took up work in the hospitals, now overflowing with the maimed and wounded.

Magenta and Solferino threw Milan into a frenzy of patriotic fervour. The popular reception accorded the French Emperor when, with his ally, Victor Emmanuel, he entered the capital of his uncle's Italian Kingdom, eclipsed all records. The aspect of the Scala opera-house during the gala performance when the Emperor, Victor Emmanuel, and the recently appointed Mayor of Milan, Count Luigi di Belgiojoso, took their places in the royal box, defied, we are told, the descriptive eloquence of the most fantastic pen.

Donna Christina rarely took part in the social festivities which were held in celebration of the expulsion of the Austrians. Accompanied by her daughter, she occasionally spent an evening amidst the kaleidoscopic host which thronged the *salon* of the Countess Maffei. Strange to say, however, she received no invitation to the Court functions held by Victor Emmanuel during his sojourn in Milan. (Barbiera, *op. cit.*) On the other hand, Cavour visited and dined with his fellow-conspirator, compensating with his genial presence for the humiliating neglect, or oversight, of the Palace officials.

The Peace of Villafranca (July, 1859), whereby Napoleon left unfulfilled his promise to free Italy from the Alps to the Adriatic, came as a staggering blow to Italian patriotism. By its stipulations Venice was abandoned to Austria. Indignant rage quickly succeeded the adulation which had been lavished by Italians on their French allies. Bitter as the deception was, it served a useful purpose.

Although the continuation of the war was abandoned, the consolidation of the advantages gained was perhaps expedited owing to Napoleon's disposition to mitigate, in so far as was consistent with political considerations nearer home, the effects of the crushing blow to Italian national aspirations. Cavour, whose despair and fury were painful to behold, threw up an office he felt he could no longer fill with profit, and to Rattazzi and the Lamarmora Ministry fell the unenviable task of bridging over the interval until the great statesman and consummate diplomatist again grasped the helm (January, 1860).

Meanwhile the crisis proved one of the most vital in the annals of the Italian struggle for unity. Once more the princess entered the lists, and placing fortune and brains at the service of her country, launched *L'Italie*, a journal which, migrating with the capital, still flourishes in Rome today. Although published in French, and intended primarily to familiarise an international public with the great political problems of Italy, the paper met with flattering local recognition, and was widely read in most Italian cities north of Rome. Strange to say its twin-sister, *L'Italia*, edited in the vernacular, soon languished and disappeared.

As our knowledge of the aspirations and tastes of its founder would lead us to infer, *L'Italie* of the early days dealt with abstruse questions affecting international politics, and was somewhat academic in tone. Problems of European Diplomacy, profusely annotated with erudite historical and technical addenda, crowd close upon dissertations on the vexed social and economic questions which confronted the legislators in Turin. The amalgamation of the fiscal systems of the new provinces, the uniformity of their judicial and forensic usages, demanded nice discrimination, all alike being jealously tenacious of established custom, and intensely susceptible where local pride or tradition was threatened.

These burning questions were treated by the princess over her own signature, and inevitably gave rise to polemics, the controversial honours of which, it must be confessed, did not always remain with her. An optimist where the future of Italy was concerned, she was frankly intolerant of the prevalent carping criticism of Cavour, whose prudent and diplomatic scheming was often wilfully misrepresented by the impulsive school which ignored France and defied Austria to do her worst.

Two pamphlets from her pen deal with the national and international political aspects of contemporaneous Europe. *Concerning Modern International Politics* is a plea for an Italian school of Diplomacy. *Observations of the Actual Condition of Italy and her Future* is an essay teeming with irrepressible optimism, which, despite many a harrowing page, demonstrates the serenity of her faith in her country's destinies. That her faith was not misplaced has been proved by the steady, although necessarily slow, intellectual, moral, and material development of the nation which made Rome its political and social capital.

Meanwhile literary occupations in nowise precluded the indulgence of her marked social proclivities. Partly on her daughter's behalf, perhaps, but certainly because of her own insatiable thirst for news and intellectual companionship, the princess's *salon* was thrown open to the *élite* of Milanese society.

Giovanni Visconti Venosta, from whose delightful memoirs, (*Ricordi di Gioventù*, Milan, 1904), we have already quoted, gives the following glimpse of the hostess:—

It was towards the close of that year (1859) that I knew the Princess Christina Belgiojoso-Trivulzio, whom I had so often heard spoken of in the past, both in my own house and among friends. She sometimes came there (to the Countess Maffei's salon), and I was introduced to her. She was most gracious to me, inviting me to her house, where I soon became a frequent visitor. When the Princess Belgiojoso entered a drawing-room all eyes were turned upon her. She was tall, but carried her head slightly bent on her breast on account of a stab she had received while in the Orient from an assassin who sought to slay her. She was then fifty years old, (in her fifty-second year), the traces of her former beauty had vanished before a premature old age; but the very large eyes preserved all their old expression.

Again, a year later, speaking of the phalanx of foreign politicians, journalists, and travellers who were attracted to Italy by the spectacle of a nation awakening to the ideals of Liberty and Independence, Visconti Venosta writes:

Of these foreigners, I met many at the house of the Princess Belgiojoso, where, nevertheless, none were welcome who presumed to doubt the final triumph of our cause, or who risked criticism derogatory to our acts or our public men. The old patriotic enthusiasm survived undiminished in the princess; and now that the old aspirations were about to become realities, she took exception with those who were not prepared to welcome their triumph. She admired our best political talent, and above all Cavour; she was intolerant of any criticism, believing it harmful at the present juncture, and not permitting any one to disturb her optimism.

An optimist myself, and furthermore free from the disillusions of mature age, we agreed perfectly in our discussions, so that in a very short time I became one of those with whom the prin-

Blevio, Lake Como

cess liked best to converse on political topics, and whom she received in the most courteous and cordial manner. When she was receiving, a *narghilé* was brought to her, and she smoked, I don't know what: but it was not tobacco. Generally, she sat at a little table and did embroidery while conversing. Sometimes she wrote holding a pad on her knees; working in the midst of animated conversations and discussions, composing pamphlets, or articles for the newspapers and reviews, especially for the *Revue des Deux Mondes*, and generally writing in French, which she said came easiest to her. When she was ill she rarely went to bed, but reclined in a great armchair, clothed and muffled up in shawls, and dosing herself, as she had a fad for medicine.—*Ricordi di Gioventù.*

Another visitor, the French diplomatist, Henry d'Ideville, thus describes his meeting with the Italian celebrity in 1859 or 1860:

I had heard a great deal about the princess, of her intelligence, her energy and her beauty, but the impression produced by this first interview was very profound. The prematurely bent figure, the flashing eye, the gravity of expression and her imperious gestures, the incisive and characteristic speech, all denoted in her a will of iron and a passionate nature.—*Journal d'un diplomate en Italie.*

The next few years were passed partly in Milan or at Locate, or, during the late summer and autumn, at her recently acquired villa on Lake Como, near Blevio. This latter abode was within a short walk of the historic Villa Pliniana, where her faithless husband passed those idyllic, if illicit, years with his paramour, the Duchess of Plaisance. But the vicinity of a spot round which clustered such painful memories would seem to have in no way disturbed the equanimity of the princess.

Among countless contributions to the daily and periodical press her pen produced an essay for the initial number of the *Nuova Antologia* (January 1, 1866), which took the place of the defunct *Antologia Italiana*, founded by her old friend and correspondent Vieusseux. Some critics find in *On the Present Condition of Women, and their Future*, evidences of a vital truth which cause them to rank it among the most able and conscientious of her sociological studies. It certainly evinces not only a deep and varied technical knowledge of her subject, but lays bare the fine personal sympathy with which the princess followed and sought to advance the efforts of those of her sex who craved emancipation from the meaningless and hampering restrictions which then beset Italian womanhood.

Arguing from the premise that "society is formed on the basis of the presumed inferiority of woman," the writer laments that in Italy reform is particularly difficult because the women themselves lend colour to this essentially false estimate of their natural endowments, owing to a national subserviency to the mediaeval prejudices and social traditions which preclude any determined effort to attain a higher intellectual plane. The princess indignantly exclaims:

> But is it not time, that the partners and mothers of the lords of creation be considered seriously as rational beings, endowed, perhaps, with specific intellectual attributes, but not necessarily inferior to those of man?

Unlike many of the advocates for Women's Rights of today, the princess puts forth no exaggerated claims for her sex. She is content to leave man in undisputed possession of most of his usurped prerogatives; but she suggests that women might advantageously study medicine. She clearly foresees serious difficulties in the achievement of even the modest ends she has in mind, yet her ineradicable optimism convinces her that Italy will solve this social problem even as she has solved so many of the intricate political and diplomatic problems which but lately confronted her.

Of the expression of her views on the relationship between Church and State, another problem already looming big on the political horizon, the princess was exceedingly reticent. Her objections to Gioberti's schemes as set forth in the *Primato* have been recorded. Her philosophy was eclecticism without originality. Imbued with a mildly scientific positivism, she trembled, notwithstanding, lest her *Essay on the Formation of the Catholic Dogma* should be placed on the *Index Librorum Prohibitorum* of the Vatican. While clinging to her intellectual independence, she suffered tortures from superstitious apprehensions, and was continually obsessed by a craven fear of death.

Yet, in a sense, she was a religious woman, although, like many an *esprit fort*, she had had her periods of irreligion, or perhaps, more correctly, of indifference towards religious matters. The fervour of her mystic devotion during the composition of the *Essay* was a psychic phase, in no way more representative of her normal attitude towards theological matters than were her spectacular audacities indicative of the sincerity of her patriotism. She was as jealous of the liberty of her religious conscience as of her political creeds.

Although the princess lived to witness the fall of the Temporal Power, this portentous event was still too close for any just appreciation of the full significance of the moral struggle which inevitably must result between Church and State. The Cavourian axiom, a Free Church in a Free State, had her unqualified sympathy. Although theoretically an ideal solution, the Hierarchy of the Vatican has persistently rejected it as incompatible with a system which clings to the exercise of political rule over a few thousand Italians as indispensable to the spiritual guidance of Christendom.

CHAPTER 15

Her death in Milan

Ninety-Nine times out of a hundred, one is tempted to draw a veil over the closing scenes of a biographical study. Alas! the most brilliant qualities of mind, the fairest charm of manner, must fade and grow pale before the inexorable advance of bodily and mental infirmities. The life of the Princess Belgiojoso is no exception. What is it, after all, that arrests and captivates our interest in the career of this exceptionally gifted woman, if not her intense intellectual and physical activity? Eye-witnesses have informed us that at fifty the princess was prematurely aged; a few years later she is so bent that when she walked a person behind her could not see her head. With advancing years came also a recrudescence of the distressing malady which had vexed her life.

Nevertheless, her *salon* continued to attract not merely old friends but strangers, eager to meet a woman of whom the world had heard so much. Barbiera says that at Milan and at Locate the princess received a strange medley of company, both illustrious and obscure, nameless foreigners and Italians boasting historic titles. Everyone was invited to dinner. To these repasts came beautiful worldlings in Court dresses, who had received their invitations, in accordance with the exigencies of strictest etiquette, a week in advance; and with them came also music-teachers, journalists, or exiles encountered during her sojourns in Paris, Athens, or Constantinople, old and young, rich and poor, who had received an off-hand bid an hour before.

The ivory shoulders of a duchess, shimmering beneath a load of diamonds, rubbed against the shabby rusty coat (buttoned to the chin, to conceal his doubtful linen) of some poor *protégée* petitioning for a mastership in one of the public schools. The ladies and gentlemen were unceremoniously grouped round his mistress by her Turkish servant, the more obscure guests gathering at the lower end of the table. The princess ate a little, and then fell asleep, upon which guests who were not accustomed to the ways of the house maintained a religious silence until the hostess, opening wide her great eyes, querulously exclaimed: "Talk; pray go on talking;" and forthwith relapsed into somnolence. When the meal was over she awoke, and, followed by all her guests, passed into the music-room, where, seated in an armchair, she stitched clothing for poor children or smoked her inevitable *narghilé*.

At the villa on Lake Como her life, at least during the earlier years of her periodical sojourns, was hardly less full than in Milan. She was constantly surrounded by friends from the fashionable world and stars of the literary, artistic, and musical circles. Her lifelong passion for the soothing delights of harmony was rivalled only by her undying enthusiasm for politics. For Verdi she professed unbounded admiration, and on more than one occasion publicly defended the great composer against the ungenerous criticism of his Milanese fellow-citizens. (Barbiera, *Passioni del Risorgimento*.)

Among her intimates at Blevio was Sophia O'Ferrall, widow of Count Confalonieri, whom the princess had so scathingly criticised in her *Studies Concerning the History of Lombardy in Recent Years*—a pamphlet, published in 1846, which excited widespread and angry comment, and was the incentive to the journey which cost the haughty patriot his life.

Gradually the circle was narrowed about the invalid, although to the last, when her strength permitted, Donna Christina eagerly welcomed friends and acquaintances, invariably seeking news of the political incidents of the day, each successive step towards the final coronation of the edifice of National Unity bringing a proud flash to her eyes and a suspicion of fleeting colour to her wasted cheek.

Only a few days before her death, Visconti Venosta found her propped up in her armchair.

> I had gone one morning to ask news of her, and hearing I was in the drawing-room, she desired to see me. Making a sign to me to approach, and intimating that she wished to speak to me, in a whisper she feebly begged for the latest news concerning—I have forgotten what—important political incident. Politics and patriotism occupied her thoughts even during the last hours of her life.—*Ricordi di Gioventù*.

Inexorably the insidious dropsical malady from which she suffered made its ravages more keenly felt. Slowly her strength failed and ebbed; the fires of her mental vigour burnt lower, till on the evening of July 5, 1871, she passed away.

She had lived to witness the crowning of the great work towards the accomplishment of which all her efforts had been directed. Italy was united under the Constitutional rule of Victor Emmanuel II., and the capital of the new nation was Rome.

The princess died in Milan, at the age of sixty-three. Her illness had precluded the annual flitting to Locate or Blevio, as was her wont at this season. It was at Locate, however, that she was laid to her final rest: without pomp, and attended only by a small band of relatives and intimate friends who had tarried on in Milan, despite the great heat, in order to pay the last tribute to one who, whatever her shortcomings, possessed not merely magnetic charm but the more enviable power of winning and retaining human affection.

The romantic chronicles of her time accord the Princess Belgiojoso conspicuous prominence. Her place in History is less assured. The passionless ethics of the modern school of historical criticism—essentially positive in application and deduction—must, perforce, look askance at the *dilettanteism* of her political career. Susceptible to emotional impulse rather than to reflective will; prone to individualism (a serious fault in the political sense of the term), her life and actions are redundant with those negative virtues which a rugged consistency alone stamps with the distinctive marks of greatness. The highly charged romantic atmosphere in which she lived, breathed, and had her being, combined with her peculiarly impressionable temperament, are advanced in extenuation of many of her follies. It were idle, however, for her biographer to urge claims which cannot be substantiated. On the other hand, of the sincerity of her devotion to the patriotic ideals she professed, her life affords ample testimony; while the dramatic picturesqueness of her career adds a colouring, we could ill spare.

An old saw has it that "the lesser saints are the ruin of God." Nevertheless, Italians discern scant risk of imperilling the sanctity of the Nation's Valhalla by according to Christina Belgiojoso a niche in the dim recesses where lie enshrined the memories of the heroes and martyrs of that National Unity towards the achievement of which her whole life was dedicated.

LEONAUR

ALSO FROM LEONAUR
AVAILABLE IN SOFTCOVER OR HARDCOVER WITH DUST JACKET

THE WOMAN IN BATTLE *by Loreta Janeta Velazquez*—Soldier, Spy and Secret Service Agent for the Confederacy During the American Civil War.

BOOTS AND SADDLES *by Elizabeth B. Custer*—The experiences of General Custer's Wife on the Western Plains.

FANNIE BEERS' CIVIL WAR *by Fannie A. Beers*—A Confederate Lady's Experiences of Nursing During the Campaigns & Battles of the American Civil War.

LADY SALE'S AFGHANISTAN *by Florentia Sale*—An Indomitable Victorian Lady's Account of the Retreat from Kabul During the First Afghan War.

THE TWO WARS OF MRS DUBERLY *by Frances Isabella Duberly*—An Intrepid Victorian Lady's Experience of the Crimea and Indian Mutiny.

THE REBELLIOUS DUCHESS *by Paul F. S. Dermoncourt*—The Adventures of the Duchess of Berri and Her Attempt to Overthrow French Monarchy.

LADIES OF WATERLOO *by Charlotte A. Eaton, Magdalene de Lancey & Juana Smith*—The Experiences of Three Women During the Campaign of 1815: Waterloo Days by Charlotte A. Eaton, A Week at Waterloo by Magdalene de Lancey & Juana's Story by Juana Smith.

NURSE AND SPY IN THE UNION ARMY *by Sarah Emma Evelyn Edmonds*—During the American Civil War

WIFE NO. 19 *by Ann Eliza Young*—The Life & Ordeals of a Mormon Woman During the 19th Century

DIARY OF A NURSE IN SOUTH AFRICA *by Alice Bron*—With the Dutch-Belgian Red Cross During the Boer War

MARIE ANTOINETTE AND THE DOWNFALL OF ROYALTY *by Imbert de Saint-Amand*—The Queen of France and the French Revolution

THE MEMSAHIB & THE MUTINY *by R. M. Coopland*—An English lady's ordeals in Gwalior and Agra duringthe Indian Mutiny 1857

MY CAPTIVITY AMONG THE SIOUX INDIANS *by Fanny Kelly*—The ordeal of a pioneer woman crossing the Western Plains in 1864

WITH MAXIMILIAN IN MEXICO *by Sara Yorke Stevenson*—A Lady's experience of the French Adventure